# Microsoft®
# Excel® 2013

Basic    Intermediate    Advanced

# Microsoft®
# Excel® 2013

Basic     Intermediate     Advanced

Elizabeth Eisner Reding/Lynn Wermers

## CENGAGE
Learning®

Australia • Brazil • Mexico • Singapore • United Kingdom • United States

**Illustrated Course Guide: Microsoft® Excel® 2013 Basic**
Elizabeth Eisner Reding/Lynn Wermers

Senior Product Manger: Marjorie Hunt

Associate Product Manager: Amanda Lyons

Senior Content Developer: Christina Kling-Garrett

Content Developer: Megan Chrisman

Marketing Manager: Gretchen Swann

Developmental Editors: Marj Hopper, Barbara Clemens

Full-Service Project Management: GEX Publishing Services

Copyeditor: Kathy Orrino

Proofreader: Brandy Lilly

Indexer: Alexandra Nickerson

QA Manuscript Reviewers: John Freitas, Jeff Schwartz, Danielle Shaw, Susan Pedicini, Susan Whalen

Print Buyer: Fola Orekoya

Cover Designer: GEX Publishing Services

Cover Artist: © Katerina Havelkova/Shutterstock

Composition: GEX Publishing Services

For product information and technology assistance, contact us at **Cengage Learning Customer & Sales Support, 1-800-354-9706**

For permission to use material from this text or product, submit all requests online at **www.cengage.com/permissions**
Further permissions questions can be emailed to **permissionrequest@cengage.com**

Library of Congress Control Number: 2013953079
ISBN-13: 978-1-285-09339-0
ISBN-10: 1-285-09339-9

**Cengage Learning**
200 First Stamford Place, 4th Floor
Stamford, CT 06902
USA

Cengage Learning is a leading provider of customized learning solutions with office locations around the globe, including Singapore, the United Kingdom, Australia, Mexico, Brazil, and Japan. Locate your local office at: **www.cengage.com/global**

Cengage Learning products are represented in Canada by Nelson Education, Ltd.

For your course and learning solutions, visit **www.cengage.com**

Purchase any of our products at your local college store or at our preferred online store **www.cengagebrain.com**

Trademarks:
Some of the product names and company names used in this book have been used for identification purposes only and may be trademarks or registered trademarks of their respective manufacturers and sellers.

Microsoft and the Windows logo are registered trademarks of Microsoft Corporation in the United States and/or other countries. Cengage Learning is an independent entity from Microsoft Corporation, and not affiliated with Microsoft in any manner.

Printed in the United States of America
1 2 3 4 5 6 7 19 18 17 16 15 14

# Brief Contents

# Contents

# Preface

Welcome to *Illustrated Course Guide: Microsoft Excel 2013 Basic*. This book has a unique design: Each skill is presented on two facing pages, with steps on the left and screens on the right. The layout makes it easy to learn a skill without having to read a lot of text and flip pages to see an illustration.

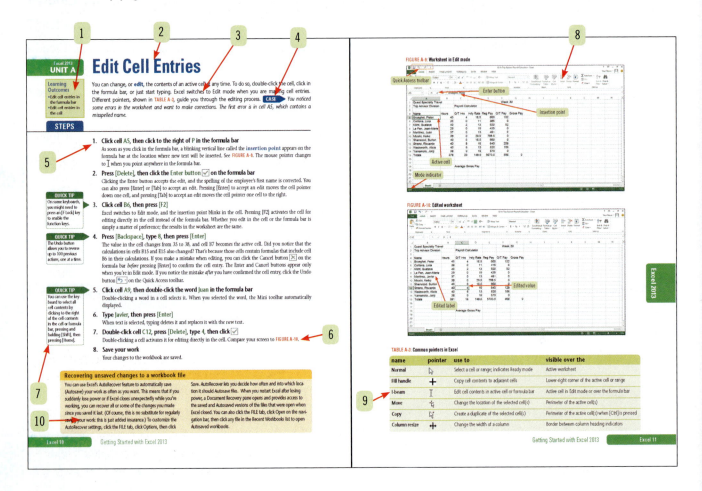

1 **New!** Learning Outcomes box lists measurable learning goals for which a student is accountable in that lesson.

2 Each two-page lesson focuses on a single skill.

3 Introduction briefly explains why the lesson skill is important.

4 A case scenario motivates the steps and puts learning in context.

5 Step-by-step instructions and brief explanations guide students through each hands-on lesson activity.

6 **New!** Figure references are now in red bold to help students refer back and forth between the steps and screenshots.

7 Tips and troubleshooting advice, right where you need it—next to the step itself.

8 **New!** Larger screenshots with green callouts keep students on track as they complete steps.

9 Tables provide summaries of helpful information such as button references or keyboard shortcuts.

10 Clues to Use yellow boxes provide useful information related to the lesson skill.

This book is an ideal learning tool for a wide range of learners—the "rookies" will find the clean design easy to follow and focused with only essential information presented, and the "hotshots" will appreciate being able to move quickly through the lessons to find the information they need without reading a lot of text. The design also makes this a great reference after the course is over! See the illustration on the left to learn more about the pedagogical and design elements of a typical lesson.

## What's New in this Edition

- **Coverage** — This book helps students learn how to use Microsoft Excel 2013 including step-by-step instructions on creating worksheets, working with formulas and functions, and creating charts. Working in the Cloud appendix helps students learn to use SkyDrive to save, share, and manage files in the cloud and to use Office Web Apps.

- **New! Learning Outcomes** — Each lesson displays a green Learning Outcomes box that lists skills-based or knowledge-based learning goals for which students are accountable. Each Learning Outcome maps to a variety of learning activities and assessments. (See the *New! Learning Outcomes* section on page xiii for more information.)

- **New! Updated Design** — This edition features many new design improvements to engage students — including larger lesson screenshots with green callouts placed on top, and a refreshed Unit Opener page.

- **New! Independent Challenge 4: Explore** — This new case-based assessment activity allows students to explore new skills and use creativity to solve a problem or create a project.

## Assignments

This book includes a wide variety of high quality assignments you can use for practice and assessment. Assignments include:

- **Concepts Review** — Multiple choice, matching, and screen identification questions.

- **Skills Review** — Step-by-step, hands-on review of every skill covered in the unit.

- **Independent Challenges 1–3** — Case projects requiring critical thinking and application of the unit skills. The Independent Challenges increase in difficulty. The first one in each unit provides the most hand-holding; the subsequent ones provide less guidance and require more critical thinking and independent problem solving.

- **Independent Challenge 4: Explore** — Case projects that let students explore new skills that are related to the core skills covered in the unit and are often more open ended, allowing students to use creativity to complete the assignment.

- **Visual Workshop** — Critical thinking exercises that require students to create a project by looking at a completed solution; they must apply the skills they've learned in the unit and use critical thinking skills to create the project from scratch.

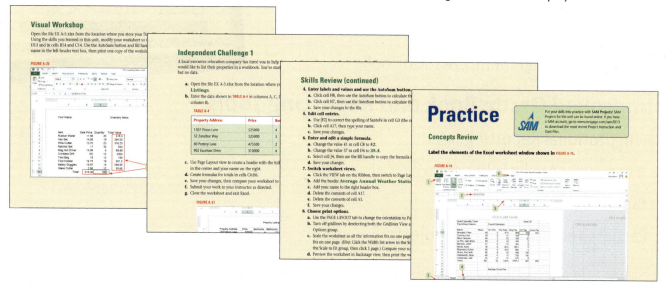

# WHAT'S NEW
## FOR SAM 2013?

Get your students workplace ready with  **SAM**

**The market-leading assessment an**
**training solution for Microsoft Offic**

## SAM 2013

### Exciting New Features and Content

➤ Computer Concepts Trainings and Assessments *(shown on monitor)*

➤ Student Assignment Calendar

➤ All New SAM Projects

➤ Mac Hints

➤ More MindTap Readers

### More Efficient Course Setup and Management Tools

➤ Individual Assignment Tool

➤ Video Playback of Student Clickpaths

➤ Express Assignment Creation Tool

### Improved Grade Book and Reporting Tools

➤ Institutional Reporting

➤ Frequency Analysis Report

➤ Grade Book Enhancements

➤ Partial Credit Grading for Projects

SAM is sold separately.

SAM's active, hands-on environment helps students master Microsoft Office skills and computer concepts that are essential to academic and career success.

 **CENGAG Learning**

# New! Learning Outcomes

Every 2-page lesson in this book now contains a green **Learning Outcomes box** that states the learning goals for that lesson.

- **What is a learning outcome?** A learning outcome states what a student is expected to know or be able to do after completing a lesson. Each learning outcome is skills-based or knowledge-based and is *measurable*. Learning outcomes map to learning activities and assessments.

- **How do students benefit from learning outcomes?** Learning outcomes tell students exactly what skills and knowledge they are *accountable* for learning in that lesson. This helps students study more efficiently and effectively and makes them more active learners.

- **How do instructors benefit from learning outcomes?** Learning outcomes provide clear, measurable, skills-based learning goals that map to various high-quality learning activities and assessments. A **Learning Outcomes Map**, available for each unit in this book, maps every learning outcome to the learning activities and assessments shown below.

## Learning Outcomes Map to These Learning Activities:

1. **Book lessons:** Step-by-step tutorial on one skill presented in a two-page learning format
2. **SAM Training:** Short animations and hands-on practice activities in simulated environment *(SAM is sold separately.)*

## Learning Outcomes Map to These Assessments:

1. **End-of-Unit Exercises: Concepts Review** (screen identification, matching, multiple choice); **Skills Review** (hands-on review of each lesson); **Independent Challenges** (hands-on, case-based review of specific skills); **Visual Workshop** (activity that requires student to build a project by looking at a picture of the final solution).
2. **Exam View Test Banks:** Objective-based questions you can use for online or paper testing.
3. **SAM Assessment:** Performance-based assessment in a simulated environment. *(SAM is sold separately.)*
4. **SAM Projects:** Auto-graded projects for Word, Excel, Access, and PowerPoint that students create. *(SAM is sold separately.)*
5. **Extra Independent Challenges:** Extra case-based exercises available in the Instructor Resources that cover various skills.

## Learning Outcomes Map

A **Learning Outcomes Map**, contained in the Instructor Resources, provides a listing of learning activities and assessments for each learning outcome in the book.

**Learning Outcomes Map**
Microsoft Excel 2013 Illustrated Complete
Unit G

**KEY:**
IC=Independent Challenge    EIC=Extra Independent Challenge
VW=Visual Workshop

| | Concepts Review | Skills Review | IC1 | IC2 | IC3 | IC4 | VW | EIC 1 | EIC 2 | Test Bank | SAM Assessment | SAM Projects | SAM Training |
|---|---|---|---|---|---|---|---|---|---|---|---|---|---|
| **Plan a table** | | | | | | | | | | | | | |
| Plan the data organization for a table | ✓ | | | ✓ | | | | | | ✓ | | | |
| Plan the data elements for a table | ✓ | | | ✓ | | | | | | ✓ | | | |
| **Create and format a table** | | | | | | | | | | | | | |
| Create a table | | ✓ | ✓ | ✓ | ✓ | ✓ | ✓ | | | ✓ | | ✓ | |
| Format a table | | ✓ | ✓ | ✓ | ✓ | ✓ | ✓ | | | ✓ | ✓ | ✓ | ✓ |
| **Add table data** | | | | | | | | | | | | | |
| Add fields to a table | | ✓ | | ✓ | ✓ | | | | | ✓ | ✓ | | ✓ |
| Add records to a table | | ✓ | ✓ | ✓ | | | | | | ✓ | ✓ | | ✓ |
| **Find and replace table data** | | | | | | | | | | | | | |
| Find data in a table | | ✓ | ✓ | | | | | | | ✓ | ✓ | ✓ | ✓ |
| Replace data in a table | | ✓ | ✓ | | ✓ | | | | | ✓ | ✓ | ✓ | ✓ |
| **Delete table data** | | | | | | | | | | | | | |
| Delete a table field | | ✓ | | | ✓ | | | | | ✓ | | | |
| Delete a table row | | ✓ | | | ✓ | | | | | ✓ | ✓ | | ✓ |
| Remove duplicate data from a table | | ✓ | ✓ | | | | | | | | | | |
| **Sort table data** | | | | | | | | | | | | | |
| Sort a table in ascending | | | | ✓ | | | | | | | | | |

# Instructor Resources

This book comes with a wide array of high-quality technology-based, teaching tools to help you teach and to help students learn. The following teaching tools are available for download at our Instructor Companion Site. Simply search for this text at *login.cengage.com*. An instructor login is required.

- **New! Learning Outcomes Map** — A detailed grid for each unit (in Excel format) shows the learning activities and assessments that map to each learning outcome in that unit.

- **Instructor's Manual** — Available as an electronic file, the Instructor's Manual includes lecture notes with teaching tips for each unit.

- **Sample Syllabus** — Prepare and customize your course easily using this sample course outline.

- **PowerPoint Presentations** — Each unit has a corresponding PowerPoint presentation covering the skills and topics in that unit that you can use in lectures, distribute to your students, or customize to suit your course.

- **Figure Files** — The figures in the text are provided on the Instructor Resources site to help you illustrate key topics or concepts. You can use these to create your own slide shows or learning tools.

- **Solution Files** — Solution Files are files that contain the finished project that students create or modify in the lessons or end-of-unit material.

- **Solutions Document** — This document outlines the solutions for the end-of-unit Concepts Review, Skills Review, Independent Challenges and Visual Workshops. An Annotated Solution File and Grading Rubric accompany each file and can be used together for efficient grading.

- **ExamView Test Banks** — ExamView is a powerful testing software package that allows you to create and administer printed, computer (LAN-based), and Internet exams. Our ExamView test banks include questions that correspond to the skills and concepts covered in this text, enabling students to generate detailed study guides that include page references for further review. The computer-based and Internet testing components allow students to take exams at their computers, and also save you time by grading each exam automatically.

## Key Facts About Using This Book

**Data Files are needed:** To complete many of the lessons and end-of-unit assignments, students need to start from partially completed Data Files, which help students learn more efficiently. By starting out with a Data File, students can focus on performing specific tasks without having to create a file from scratch. All Data Files are available as part of the Instructor Resources. Students can also download Data Files themselves for free at cengagebrain.com. (For detailed instructions, go to www.cengage.com/ct/studentdownload.)

**System requirements:** This book was developed using Microsoft Office 2013 Professional running on Windows 8. Note that Windows 8 is not a requirement for the units on Microsoft Office; Office 2013 runs virtually the same on Windows 7 and Windows 8. Please see Important Notes for Windows 7 Users on the next page for more information.

**Screen resolution:** This book was written and tested on computers with monitors set at a resolution of 1366 x 768. If your screen shows more or less information than the figures in this book, your monitor is probably set at a higher or lower resolution. If you don't see something on your screen, you might have to scroll down or up to see the object identified in the figure.

## Tell Us What You Think!

We want to hear from you! Please email your questions, comments, and suggestions to the Illustrated Series team at: **illustratedseries@cengage.com**

# Important Notes for Windows 7 Users

The screenshots in this book show Microsoft Office 2013 running on Windows 8. However, if you are using Microsoft Windows 7, you can still use this book because Office 2013 runs virtually the same on both platforms. There are only two differences that you will encounter if you are using Windows 7. Read this section to understand the differences.

## Dialog boxes

If you are a Windows 7 user, dialog boxes shown in this book will look slightly different than what you see on your screen. Dialog boxes for Windows 7 have a light blue title bar, instead of a medium blue title bar. However, beyond this superficial difference in appearance, the options in the dialog boxes across platforms are the same. For instance, the screen shots below show the Font dialog box running on Windows 7 and the Font dialog box running on Windows 8.

FIGURE 1: Font dialog box in Windows 7

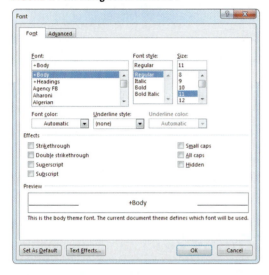

FIGURE 2: Font dialog box in Windows 8

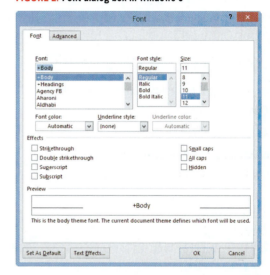

## Alternate Steps for Starting an App in Windows 7

Nearly all of the steps in this book work exactly the same for Windows 7 users. However, starting an app (or program/application) requires different steps for Windows 7. The steps below show the Windows 7 steps for starting an app. (Note: Windows 7 alternate steps also appear in red Trouble boxes next to any step in the book that requires starting an app.)

**Starting an app (or program/application) using Windows 7**

1. Click the **Start button** on the taskbar to open the Start menu.
2. Click **All Programs**, then click the **Microsoft Office 2013 folder**. See Figure 3.
3. Click the app you want to use (such as **Excel 2013**).

FIGURE 3: Starting an app using Windows 7

# Acknowledgements

## Author Acknowledgements

Creating a book of this magnitude is a team effort. I would like to thank my husband, Michael, as well as Christina Kling-Garrett, the project manager, and my development editor, Marj Hopper, for her suggestions and corrections. I would also like to thank the production and editorial staff for all their hard work that made this project a reality.

**–Elizabeth Eisner Reding**

Thanks to Barbara Clemens for her insightful contributions, invaluable feedback, great humor, and patience. Thanks also to Christina Kling-Garrett for her encouragement and support in guiding and managing this project.

**–Lynn Wermers**

## Advisory Board Acknowledgements

We thank our Illustrated Advisory Board who gave us their opinions and guided our decisions as we developed all of the new editions for Microsoft Office 2013.

**Merlin Amirtharaj**, Stanly Community College

**Londo Andrews**, J. Sargeant Reynolds Community College

**Rachelle Hall**, Glendale Community College

**Terri Helfand**, Chaffey Community College

**Sheryl Lenhart**, Terra Community College

**Dr. Jose Nieves**, Lord Fairfax Community College

## Illustrated Course Guides for Microsoft Office 2013

| | |
|---|---|
| *Illustrated Course Guide: Microsoft Word 2013 Basic* | 978-1-285-09336-9 |
| *Illustrated Course Guide: Microsoft Word 2013 Intermediate* | 978-1-285-09337-6 |
| *Illustrated Course Guide: Microsoft Word 2013 Advanced* | 978-1-285-09338-3 |
| *Illustrated Course Guide: Microsoft Excel 2013 Basic* | 978-1-285-09339-0 |
| *Illustrated Course Guide: Microsoft Excel 2013 Intermediate* | 978-1-285-09340-6 |
| *Illustrated Course Guide: Microsoft Excel 2013 Advanced* | 978-1-285-09341-3 |
| *Illustrated Course Guide: Microsoft Access 2013 Basic* | 978-1-285-09342-0 |
| *Illustrated Course Guide: Microsoft Access 2013 Intermediate* | 978-1-285-09343-7 |
| *Illustrated Course Guide: Microsoft Access 2013 Advanced* | 978-1-285-09344-4 |
| *Illustrated Course Guide: Microsoft PowerPoint 2013 Basic* | 978-1-285-09345-1 |
| *Illustrated Course Guide: Microsoft PowerPoint 2013 Advanced* | 978-1-285-09346-8 |

# Getting Started with Microsoft Office 2013

**CASE** This unit introduces you to the most frequently used programs in Office, as well as common features they all share.

## Unit Objectives

After completing this unit, you will be able to:

- Understand the Office 2013 suite
- Start an Office app
- Identify Office 2013 screen elements
- Create and save a file
- Open a file and save it with a new name
- View and print your work
- Get Help, close a file, and exit an app

### File You Will Need

OFFICE A-1.xlsx

# Understand the Office 2013 Suite

**Learning Outcomes**
• Identify Office suite components
• Describe the features of each program

Microsoft Office 2013 is a group of programs--which are also called applications or apps--designed to help you create documents, collaborate with coworkers, and track and analyze information. You use different Office programs to accomplish specific tasks, such as writing a letter or producing a presentation, yet all the programs have a similar look and feel. Microsoft Office 2013 apps feature a common, context-sensitive user interface, so you can get up to speed faster and use advanced features with greater ease. The Office apps are bundled together in a group called a **suite**. The Office suite is available in several configurations, but all include Word, Excel, and PowerPoint. Other configurations include Access, Outlook, Publisher, and other programs. **CASE** ▸ *As part of your job, you need to understand how each Office app is best used to complete specific tasks.*

## DETAILS

### The Office apps covered in this book include:

- ### Microsoft Word 2013

  When you need to create any kind of text-based document, such as a memo, newsletter, or multipage report, Word is the program to use. You can easily make your documents look great by inserting eye-catching graphics and using formatting tools such as themes, which are available in most Office programs. **Themes** are predesigned combinations of color and formatting attributes you can apply to a document. The Word document shown in **FIGURE A-1** was formatted with the Organic theme.

- ### Microsoft Excel 2013

  Excel is the perfect solution when you need to work with numeric values and make calculations. It puts the power of formulas, functions, charts, and other analytical tools into the hands of every user, so you can analyze sales projections, calculate loan payments, and present your findings in a professional manner. The Excel worksheet shown in **FIGURE A-1** tracks personal expenses. Because Excel automatically recalculates results whenever a value changes, the information is always up to date. A chart illustrates how the monthly expenses are broken down.

- ### Microsoft PowerPoint 2013

  Using PowerPoint, it's easy to create powerful presentations complete with graphics, transitions, and even a soundtrack. Using professionally designed themes and clip art, you can quickly and easily create dynamic slide shows such as the one shown in **FIGURE A-1**.

- ### Microsoft Access 2013

  Access is a relational database program that helps you keep track of large amounts of quantitative data, such as product inventories or employee records. The form shown in **FIGURE A-1** was created for a grocery store inventory database. Employees use the form to enter data about each item. Using Access enables employees to quickly find specific information such as price and quantity.

### Microsoft Office has benefits beyond the power of each program, including:

- ### Common user interface: Improving business processes

  Because the Office suite programs have a similar **interface**, or look and feel, your experience using one program's tools makes it easy to learn those in the other programs. In addition, Office documents are **compatible** with one another, meaning that you can easily incorporate, or **integrate**, an Excel chart into a PowerPoint slide, or an Access table into a Word document.

- ### Collaboration: Simplifying how people work together

  Office recognizes the way people do business today, and supports the emphasis on communication and knowledge sharing within companies and across the globe. All Office programs include the capability to incorporate feedback—called **online collaboration**—across the Internet or a company network.

**FIGURE A-1:** Microsoft Office 2013 documents

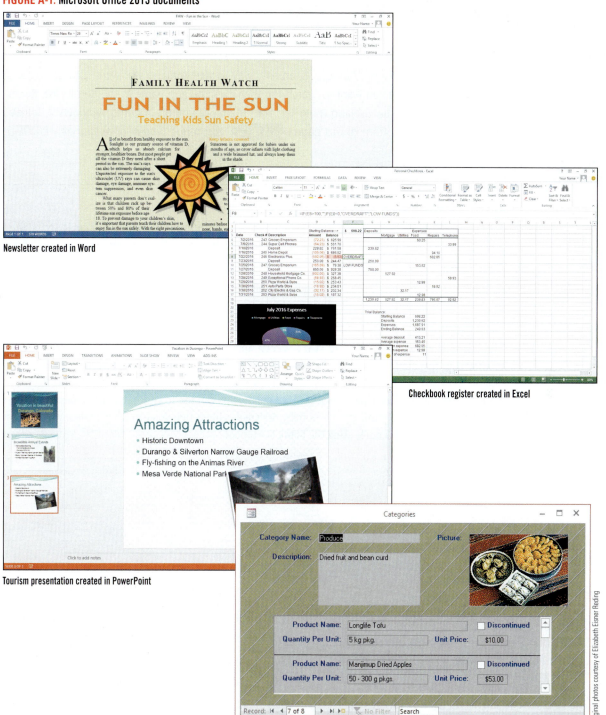

Newsletter created in Word

Checkbook register created in Excel

Tourism presentation created in PowerPoint

Store inventory form created in Access

Office 2013

## What is Office 365?

Until the release of Microsoft Office 2013, most consumers purchased Microsoft Office in a traditional way: by buying a retail package from a store or downloading it from Microsoft.com.  You can still purchase Microsoft Office 2013 in this traditional way--but you can also now purchase it as a subscription service called Microsoft Office 365 (for businesses) and

Microsoft Office 365 Home Premium (for consumers). Office 365 requires businesses to pay a subscription fee for each user. Office 365 Home Premium Edition allows households to install Office on up to 5 devices. These subscription versions of Office provide extra services and are optimized for working in the cloud.

# Start an Office App

**Learning Outcomes**
• Start an Office app
• Explain the purpose of a template
• Start a new blank document

To get started using Microsoft Office, you need to start, or **launch**, the Office app you want to use. If you are running Microsoft Office on Windows 8, an easy way to start the app you want is to go to the Start screen, type the app name you want to search for, then click the app name In the Results list. If you are running Windows 7, you start an app using the Start menu. (If you are running Windows 7, follow the Windows 7 steps at the bottom of this page.) **CASE** ▶ *You decide to familiarize yourself with Office by starting Microsoft Word.*

## STEPS

1. **Go to the Windows 8 Start screen**

   Your screen displays a variety of colorful tiles for all the apps on your computer. You could locate the app you want to open by scrolling to the right until you see it, or you can type the app name to search for it.

2. **Type word**

   Your screen now displays "Word 2013" under "Results for 'word'", along with any other app that has "word" as part of its name (such as WordPad). See **FIGURE A-2**.

3. **Click Word 2013**

   Word 2013 launches, and the Word **start screen** appears, as shown in **FIGURE A-3**. The start screen is a landing page that appears when you first start an Office app. The left side of this screen displays recent files you have opened. (If you have never opened any files, then there will be no files listed under Recent.) The right side displays images depicting different templates you can use to create different types of documents. A **template** is a file containing professionally designed content that you can easily replace with your own. You can also start from scratch using the Blank Document option.

### Starting an app using Windows 7

1. **Click the Start button ⊕ on the taskbar**
2. **Click All Programs on the Start menu, click the Microsoft Office 2013 folder as shown in FIGURE A-4, then click Word 2013**

Word 2013 launches, and the Word start screen appears, as shown previously in **FIGURE A-3**. The start screen is a landing page that appears when you first start an Office app. The left side of this screen displays recent files you have opened. (If you have never opened any files, then there will be no files listed under Recent.) The right side displays images depicting different templates you can use to create different types of documents. A **template** is a file containing professionally designed content that you can easily replace with your own. Using a template to create a document can save time and ensure that your document looks great. You can also start from scratch using the Blank Document option.

### Using shortcut keys to move between Office programs

You can switch between open apps using a keyboard shortcut. The [Alt][Tab] keyboard combination lets you either switch quickly to the next open program or file or choose one from a gallery. To switch immediately to the next open program or file, press [Alt][Tab]. To choose from all open programs and files, press and hold [Alt], then press and release [Tab] without releasing [Alt]. A gallery opens on screen, displaying the filename and a thumbnail image of each open program and file, as well as of the desktop. Each time you press [Tab] while holding [Alt], the selection cycles to the next open file or location. Release [Alt] when the program, file, or location you want to activate is selected.

**FIGURE A-2:** Searching for Word app from the Start screen in Windows 8

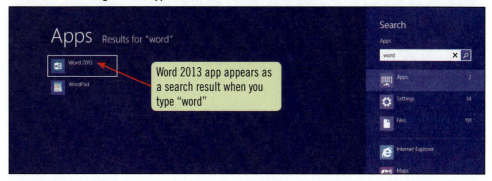

Word 2013 app appears as a search result when you type "word"

**FIGURE A-3:** Word start screen

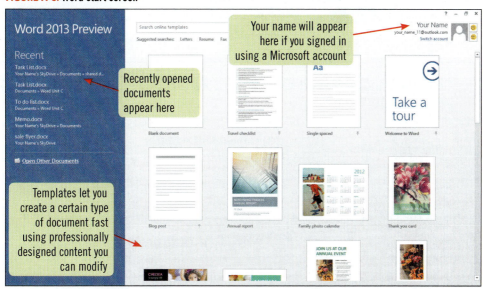

Your name will appear here if you signed in using a Microsoft account

Recently opened documents appear here

Templates let you create a certain type of document fast using professionally designed content you can modify

**FIGURE A-4:** Starting an app using Windows 7

## Using the Office Clipboard

You can use the Office Clipboard to cut and copy items from one Office program and paste them into others. The Office Clipboard can store a maximum of 24 items. To access it, open the Office Clipboard task pane by clicking the dialog box launcher 🖾 in the Clipboard group on the HOME tab. Each time you copy a selection, it is saved in the Office Clipboard. Each entry in the Office Clipboard includes an icon that tells you the program it was created in. To paste an entry, click in the document where you want it to appear, then click the item in the Office Clipboard. To delete an item from the Office Clipboard, right-click the item, then click Delete.

Office 2013

**Learning Outcomes**
- Identify basic components of the user interface
- Display and use Backstage view
- Adjust the Zoom level

# Identify Office 2013 Screen Elements

One of the benefits of using Office is that the programs have much in common, making them easy to learn and making it simple to move from one to another. Individual Office programs have always shared many features, but the innovations in the Office 2013 user interface mean even greater similarity among them all. That means you can also use your knowledge of one program to get up to speed in another. A **user interface** is a collective term for all the ways you interact with a software program. The user interface in Office 2013 provides intuitive ways to choose commands, work with files, and navigate in the program window.  **CASE** ▷ *Familiarize yourself with some of the common interface elements in Office by examining the PowerPoint program window.*

## STEPS

**TROUBLE**

If you are running WIndows 7, click the Start button on the taskbar, type **power**, then click PowerPoint 2013.

1. **Go to the Windows 8 Start screen, type pow, click PowerPoint 2013, then click Blank Presentation**

   PowerPoint becomes the active program displaying a blank slide. Refer to **FIGURE A-5** to identify common elements of the Office user interface. The **document window** occupies most of the screen. At the top of every Office program window is a **title bar** that displays the document name and program name. Below the title bar is the **Ribbon**, which displays commands you're likely to need for the current task. Commands are organized onto **tabs**. The tab names appear at the top of the Ribbon, and the active tab appears in front.

**QUICK TIP**

The Ribbon in every Office program includes tabs specific to the program, but all Office programs include a FILE tab and HOME tab on the left end of the Ribbon. Just above the FILE tab is the **Quick Access toolbar**, which also includes buttons for common Office commands.

2. **Click the FILE tab**

   The FILE tab opens, displaying **Backstage view**. It is called Backstage view becausee the commands available here are for working with the files "behind the scenes." The navigation bar on the left side of Backstage view contains commands to perform actions common to most Office programs.

3. **Click the Back button ⬅ to close Backstage view and return to the document window, then click the DESIGN tab on the Ribbon**

   To display a different tab, click its name. Each tab contains related commands arranged into **groups** to make features easy to find. On the DESIGN tab, the Themes group displays available design themes in a **gallery**, or visual collection of choices you can browse. Many groups contain a **dialog box launcher**, which you can click to open a dialog box or pane from which to choose related commands.

4. **Move the mouse pointer ⫝ over the Ion theme in the Themes group as shown in FIGURE A-6, but *do not click* the mouse button**

   The Ion theme is temporarily applied to the slide in the document window. However, because you did not click the theme, you did not permanently change the slide. With the **Live Preview** feature, you can point to a choice, see the results, then decide if you want to make the change. Live Preview is available throughout Office.

**TROUBLE**

If you accidentally click a theme, click the Undo button on the Quick Access toolbar.

5. **Move ⫝ away from the Ribbon and towards the slide**

   If you had clicked the Ion theme, it would be applied to this slide. Instead, the slide remains unchanged.

**QUICK TIP**

You can also use the Zoom button in the Zoom group on the VIEW tab to enlarge or reduce a document's appearance.

6. **Point to the Zoom slider** ━━━━┃━━━━╋ 100% **on the status bar, then drag to the right until the Zoom level reads 166%**

   The slide display is enlarged. Zoom tools are located on the status bar. You can drag the slider or click the Zoom In or Zoom Out buttons to zoom in or out on an area of interest. **Zooming in** (a higher percentage), makes a document appear bigger on screen but less of it fits on the screen at once; **zooming out** (a lower percentage) lets you see more of the document at a reduced size.

7. **Click the Zoom Out button ▬ on the status bar to the left of the Zoom slider until the Zoom level reads 120%**

**FIGURE A-5:** PowerPoint program window

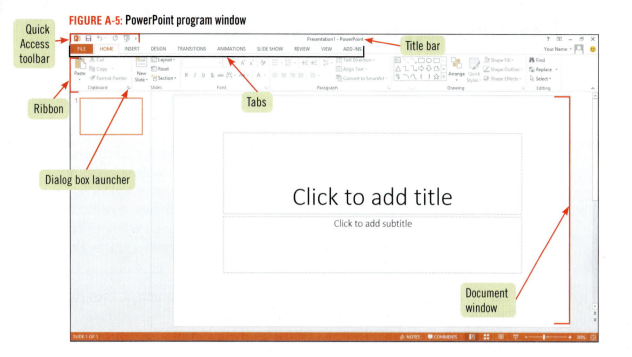

Quick Access toolbar

Ribbon

Dialog box launcher

Title bar

Tabs

Document window

**FIGURE A-6:** Viewing a theme with Live Preview

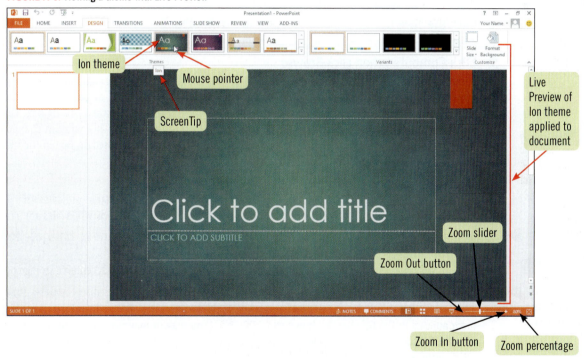

Ion theme

Mouse pointer

ScreenTip

Live Preview of Ion theme applied to document

Zoom slider

Zoom Out button

Zoom In button

Zoom percentage

---

## Using Backstage view

**Backstage view** in each Microsoft Office program offers "one stop shopping" for many commonly performed tasks, such as opening and saving a file, printing and previewing a document, defining document properties, sharing information, and exiting a program. Backstage view opens when you click the FILE tab in any Office program, and while features such as the Ribbon, Mini toolbar, and Live Preview all help you work *in* your documents, the FILE tab and Backstage view help you work *with* your documents. You can return to your active document by pressing the Back button.

# Create and Save a File

When working in an Office program, one of the first things you need to do is to create and save a file. A **file** is a stored collection of data. Saving a file enables you to work on a project now, then put it away and work on it again later. In some Office programs, including Word, Excel, and PowerPoint, you can open a new file when you start the program, then all you have to do is enter some data and save it. In Access, you must create a file before you enter any data. You should give your files meaningful names and save them in an appropriate location, such as a folder on your hard drive or SkyDrive so they're easy to find. **SkyDrive** is the Microsoft cloud storage system that lets you easily save, share, and access your files from anywhere you have Internet access. See "Saving Files to SkyDrive" for more information on this topic. **CASE** *Use Word to familiarize yourself with creating and saving a document. First you'll type some notes about a possible location for a corporate meeting, then you'll save the information for later use.*

## STEPS

1. **Click the Word program button 🪟 on the taskbar, click Blank document, then click the Zoom In button ➕ until the level is 120%, if necessary**

2. **Type Locations for Corporate Meeting, then press [Enter] twice**
   The text appears in the document window, and the **insertion point** blinks on a new blank line. The insertion point indicates where the next typed text will appear.

3. **Type Las Vegas, NV, press [Enter], type San Diego, CA, press [Enter], type Seattle, WA, press [Enter] twice, then type your name**

4. **Click the Save button 💾 on the Quick Access toolbar**
   Backstage view opens showing various options for saving the file, as shown in **FIGURE A-7**.

5. **Click Computer, then click Browse**
   Because this is the first time you are saving this document, the Save As command is displayed. Once you choose a location where you will save the file, the Save As dialog box displays, as shown in **FIGURE A-8**. Once a file is saved, clicking 💾 saves any changes to the file *without* opening the Save As dialog box. The Address bar in the Save As dialog box displays the default location for saving the file, but you can change it to any location. The File name field contains a suggested name for the document based on text in the file, but you can enter a different name.

6. **Type OF A-Potential Corporate Meeting Locations**
   The text you type replaces the highlighted text. (The "OF A-" in the filename indicates that the file is created in Office Unit A. You will see similar designations throughout this book when files are named.)

7. **In the Save As dialog box, use the Address bar or Navigation Pane to navigate to the location where you store your Data Files**
   You can store files on your computer, a network drive, your SkyDrive, or any acceptable storage device.

8. **Click Save**
   The Save As dialog box closes, the new file is saved to the location you specified, and the name of the document appears in the title bar, as shown in **FIGURE A-9**. (You may or may not see the file extension ".docx" after the filename.) See **TABLE A-1** for a description of the different types of files you create in Office, and the file extensions associated with each.

**TABLE A-1:** Common filenames and default file extensions

| file created in | is called a | and has the default extension |
| --- | --- | --- |
| Word | document | .docx |
| Excel | workbook | .xlsx |
| PowerPoint | presentation | .pptx |
| Access | database | .accdb |

© 2014 Cengage Learning

**FIGURE A-7:** Save As screen in Backstage view

Saves to your SkyDrive account

Click to save to your computer or alternate storage device

Click to change location for file

**FIGURE A-8:** Save As dialog box

Address bar

Navigation pane; your links and folders may differ

File name field; your computer may not display file extensions

Save as type list

**FIGURE A-9:** Saved and named Word document

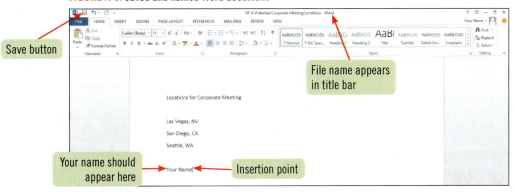

Save button

File name appears in title bar

Your name should appear here

Insertion point

## Saving files to SkyDrive

All Office programs include the capability to incorporate feedback—called **online collaboration**—across the Internet or a company network. Using **cloud computing** (work done in a virtual environment), you can take advantage of commonly shared features such as a consistent interface. Using SkyDrive, a free file storage service from Microsoft, you and your colleagues can create and store documents in the cloud and make the documents available anywhere there is Internet access to whomever you choose. To use SkyDrive, you need a free Microsoft Account, which you obtain at the signup.live.com website. You can find more information about SkyDrive in the "Working in the Cloud" appendix. When you are logged into your Microsoft account and you save a file in any of the Office apps, the first option in the Save As screen is your SkyDrive. Double-click your SkyDrive option and the Save As dialog box opens displaying a location in the address bar unique to your SkyDrive account. Type a name in the File name text box, then click Save and your file is saved to your SkyDrive. To sync your files with SkyDrive, you'll need to download and install the SkyDrive for Windows app. Then, when you open Explorer, you'll notice a new folder called SkyDrive has been added to the Users folder. In this folder is a sub-folder called Documents, in which an updated copy of your Office app files resides. This means if your Internet connection fails, you can work on your files offline. The SkyDrive folder also displays Explorer in the list of Favorites folders.

Office 2013

# Open a File and Save It with a New Name

In many cases as you work in Office, you start with a blank document, but often you need to use an existing file. It might be a file you or a coworker created earlier as a work in progress, or it could be a complete document that you want to use as the basis for another. For example, you might want to create a budget for this year using the budget you created last year; instead of typing in all the categories and information from scratch, you could open last year's budget, save it with a new name, and just make changes to update it for the current year. By opening the existing file and saving it with the Save As command, you create a duplicate that you can modify to suit your needs, while the original file remains intact. **CASE** ▸ *Use Excel to open an existing workbook file, and save it with a new name so the original remains unchanged.*

## STEPS

1. **Go to the Windows 8 Start screen, type exc, click Excel 2013, click Open Other Workbooks, click Computer on the navigation bar, then click Browse**

   The Open dialog box opens, where you can navigate to any drive or folder accessible to your computer to locate a file. You can click Recent Workbooks on the navigation bar to display a list of recent workbooks; click a file in the list to open it.

2. **In the Open dialog box, navigate to the location where you store your Data Files**

   The files available in the current folder are listed, as shown in **FIGURE A-10**. This folder displays one file.

3. **Click OFFICE A-1.xlsx, then click Open**

   The dialog box closes, and the file opens in Excel. An Excel file is an electronic spreadsheet, so the new file displays a grid of rows and columns you can use to enter and organize data.

4. **Click the FILE tab, click Save As on the navigation bar, then click Browse**

   The Save As dialog box opens, and the current filename is highlighted in the File name text box. Using the Save As command enables you to create a copy of the current, existing file with a new name. This action preserves the original file and creates a new file that you can modify.

5. **Navigate to the location where you store your Data Files if necessary, type OF A-Budget for Corporate Meeting in the File name text box, as shown in FIGURE A-11, then click Save**

   A copy of the existing workbook is created with the new name. The original file, Office A-1.xlsx, closes automatically.

6. **Click cell A19, type your name, then press [Enter], as shown in FIGURE A-12**

   In Excel, you enter data in cells, which are formed by the intersection of a row and a column. Cell A19 is at the intersection of column A and row 19. When you press [Enter], the cell pointer moves to cell A20.

7. **Click the Save button 🔲 on the Quick Access toolbar**

   Your name appears in the workbook, and your changes to the file are saved.

### Exploring File Open options

You might have noticed that the Open button in the Open dialog box includes a list arrow to the right of the button. In a dialog box, if a button includes a list arrow you can click the button to invoke the command, or you can click the list arrow to see a list of related commands that you can apply to a selected file in the file list. The Open list arrow includes several related commands, including Open Read-Only and Open as Copy.

Clicking Open Read-Only opens a file that you can only save with a new name; you cannot make changes to the original file. Clicking Open as Copy creates and opens a copy of the selected file and inserts the word "Copy" in the file's title. Like the Save As command, these commands provide additional ways to use copies of existing files while ensuring that original files do not get changed by mistake.

**FIGURE A-10:** Open dialog box

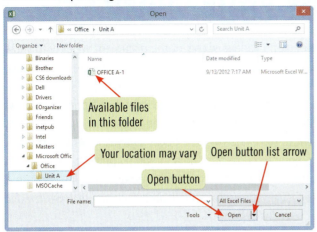

Available files in this folder

Your location may vary

Open button list arrow

Open button

**FIGURE A-11:** Save As dialog box

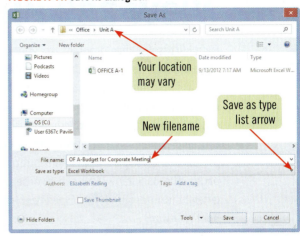

Your location may vary

Save as type list arrow

New filename

**FIGURE A-12:** Your name added to the workbook

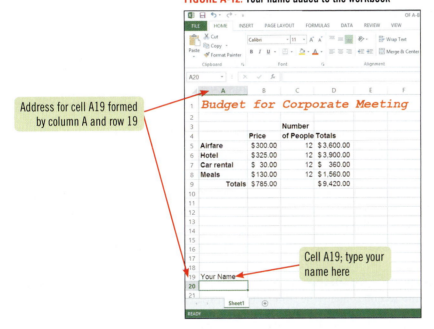

Address for cell A19 formed by column A and row 19

Cell A19; type your name here

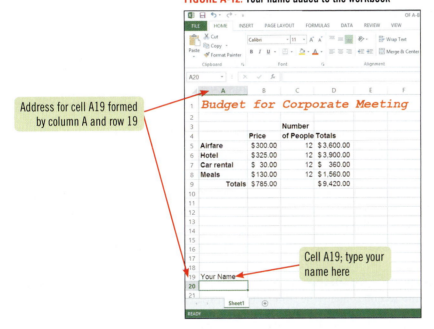

## Working in Compatibility Mode

Not everyone upgrades to the newest version of Office. As a general rule, new software versions are **backward compatible**, meaning that documents saved by an older version can be read by newer software. To open documents created in older Office versions, Office 2013 includes a feature called Compatibility Mode. When you use Office 2013 to open a file created in an earlier version of Office, "Compatibility Mode" appears in the title bar, letting you know the file was created in an earlier but usable version of the program. If you are working with someone who may not be using the newest version of the software, you can avoid possible incompatibility problems by saving your file in another, earlier format. To do this in an Office program, click the FILE tab, click Save As on the navigation bar, click the location where you want to save the file, then click Browse. In the Save As dialog box, click the Save as type list arrow in the Save As dialog box, then click an option on the list. For example, if you're working in Excel, click Excel 97-2003 Workbook format in the Save as type list to save an Excel file so it can be opened in Excel 97 or Excel 2003.

# View and Print Your Work

**Learning Outcomes**
• Describe and change views in an app
• Print a document

Each Microsoft Office program lets you switch among various **views** of the document window to show more or fewer details or a different combination of elements that make it easier to complete certain tasks, such as formatting or reading text. Changing your view of a document does not affect the file in any way, it affects only the way it looks on screen. If your computer is connected to a printer or a print server, you can easily print any Office document using the Print button on the Print tab in Backstage view. Printing can be as simple as **previewing** the document to see exactly what a document will look like when it is printed and then clicking the Print button. Or, you can customize the print job by printing only selected pages. The Backstage view can also be used to share your document with others, or to export it in a different format. **CASE** ▶ *Experiment with changing your view of a Word document, and then preview and print your work.*

## STEPS

1. **Click the Word program button** ⬛ **on the taskbar**

   Word becomes the active program, and the document fills the screen.

**QUICK TIP**
To minimize the display of the buttons and commands on tabs, click the Collapse the Ribbon button ⟩ on the lower-right end of the Ribbon.

2. **Click the VIEW tab on the Ribbon**

   In most Office programs, the VIEW tab on the Ribbon includes groups and commands for changing your view of the current document. You can also change views using the View buttons on the status bar.

3. **Click the Read Mode button in the Views group on the VIEW tab**

   The view changes to Read Mode view, as shown in **FIGURE A-13**. This view shows the document in an easy-to-read, distraction-free reading mode. Notice that the Ribbon is no longer visible on screen.

4. **Click the Print Layout button** ⬛ **on the Status bar**

   You return to Print Layout view, the default view in Word.

5. **Click the FILE tab, then click Print on the navigation bar**

   The Print tab opens in Backstage view. The preview pane on the right side of the window displays a preview of how your document will look when printed. Compare your screen to **FIGURE A-14**. Options in the Settings section enable you to change margins, orientation, and paper size before printing. To change a setting, click it, and then click a new setting. For instance, to change from Letter paper size to Legal, click Letter in the Settings section, then click Legal on the menu that opens. The document preview updates as you change the settings. You also can use the Settings section to change which pages to print. If your computer is connected to multiple printers, you can click the current printer in the Printer section, then click the one you want to use. The Print section contains the Print button and also enables you to select the number of copies of the document to print.

**QUICK TIP**
You can add the Quick Print button 🖨 to the Quick Access toolbar by clicking the Customize Quick Access Toolbar button, then clicking Quick Print. The Quick Print button prints one copy of your document using the default settings.

6. **If your school allows printing, click the Print button in the Print section (otherwise, click the Back button** ⬅ **)**

   If you chose to print, a copy of the document prints, and Backstage view closes.

---

### Customizing the Quick Access toolbar

You can customize the Quick Access toolbar to display your favorite commands. To do so, click the Customize Quick Access Toolbar button ⬇ in the title bar, then click the command you want to add. If you don't see the command in the list, click More Commands to open the Quick Access Toolbar tab of the current program's Options dialog box. In the Options dialog box, use the Choose commands from list to choose a category, click the desired command in the list on the left, click Add to add it to the Quick Access toolbar, then click OK. To remove a button from the toolbar, click the name in the list on the right in the Options dialog box, then click Remove. To add a command to the Quick Access toolbar as you work, simply right-click the button on the Ribbon, then click Add to Quick Access Toolbar on the shortcut menu. To move the Quick Access toolbar below the Ribbon, click the Customize Quick Access Toolbar button, and then click Show Below the Ribbon.

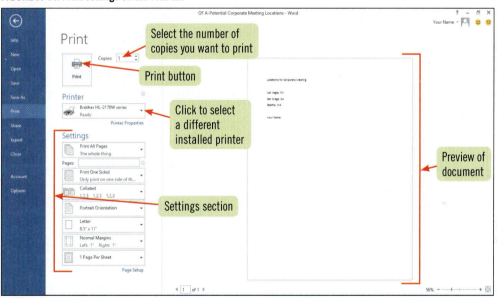

## Creating a screen capture

A **screen capture** is a digital image of your screen, as if you took a picture of it with a camera. For instance, you might want to take a screen capture if an error message occurs and you want a Technical Support person to see exactly what's on the screen. You can create a screen capture using features found in Windows 8 or Office 2013. Both Windows 7 and Windows 8 come with the Snipping Tool, a separate program designed to capture whole screens or portions of screens. To open the Snipping Tool, click the Start screen thumbnail, type "sni", then click the Snipping Tool when it appears in the left panel. After opening the Snipping Tool, click New, then drag the pointer on the screen to select the area of the screen you want to capture. When you release the mouse button, the screen capture opens in the Snipping Tool window, and you can save, copy, or send it in an email. In Word, Excel, and PowerPoint 2013, you can capture screens or portions of screens and insert them in the current document using the Screenshot button in the Illustrations group on the INSERT tab. And finally, you can create a screen capture by pressing [PrtScn]. (Keyboards differ, but you may find the [PrtScn] button in or near your keyboard's function keys.) Pressing this key places a digital image of your screen in the Windows temporary storage area known as the **Clipboard**. Open the document where you want the screen capture to appear, click the HOME tab on the Ribbon (if necessary), then click the Paste button in the Clipboard group on the HOME tab. The screen capture is pasted into the document.

# Get Help, Close a File, and Exit an App

You can get comprehensive help at any time by pressing [F1] in an Office app or clicking the Help button on the right end of the title bar. You can also get help in the form of a ScreenTip by pointing to almost any icon in the program window. When you're finished working in an Office document, you have a few choices regarding ending your work session. You close a file by clicking the FILE tab, then clicking Close; you exit a program by clicking the Close button on the title bar. Closing a file leaves a program running, while exiting a program closes all the open files in that program as well as the program itself. In all cases, Office reminds you if you try to close a file or exit a program and your document contains unsaved changes. **CASE** *Explore the Help system in Microsoft Office, and then close your documents and exit any open programs.*

## STEPS

1. **Point to the Zoom button in the Zoom group on the VIEW tab of the Ribbon**
   A ScreenTip appears that describes how the Zoom button works and explains where to find other zoom controls.

2. **Click the Microsoft Word Help (F1) button ? in the upper-right corner of the title bar**
   The Word Help window opens, as shown in **FIGURE A-15**, displaying the home page for help in Word. Each entry is a hyperlink you can click to open a list of topics. The Help window also includes a toolbar of useful Help commands such as printing and increasing the font size for easier readability, and a Search field. If you are not connected to Office.com, a gold band is displayed telling you that you are not connected. Office.com supplements the help content available on your computer with a wide variety of up-to-date topics, templates, and training. If you are not connected to the Internet, the Help window displays only the help content available on your computer.

3. **Click the Learn Word basics link in the Getting started section of the Word Help window**
   The Word Help window changes, and a list of basic tasks appears below the topic.

4. **If necessary, scroll down until the Choose a template topic fills the Word Help window**
   The topic is displayed in the pane of the Help window, as shown in **FIGURE A-16**. The content in the window explains that you can create a document using a template (a pre-formatted document) or just create a blank document.

5. **Click in the Search online help text box, type Delete, then press [Enter]**
   The Word Help window now displays a list of links to topics about different types of deletions that are possible within Word.

6. **Click the Keep Help on Top button 📌 in the upper-right corner (below the Close button)**
   The Pin Help button rotates so the pin point is pointed towards the bottom of the screen: this allows you to read the Help window while you work on your document.

7. **Click the Word document window, then notice the Help window remains visible**

8. **Click a blank area of the Help window, click 📌 to Unpin Help, click the Close button ✖ in the Help window, then click the Close button ✖ in the upper-right corner of the screen**
   Word closes, and the Excel program window is active.

9. **Click the Close button ✖ to exit Excel, click the Close button ✖ to exit the remaining Excel workbook, click the PowerPoint program button 📄 on the taskbar if necessary, then click the Close button ✖ to exit PowerPoint**
   Excel and PowerPoint both close.

**FIGURE A-15:** Word Help window

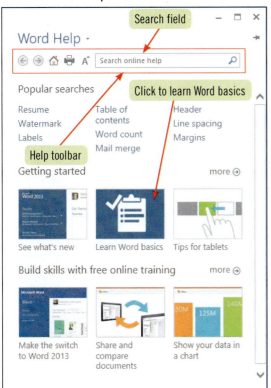

Search field

Click to learn Word basics

Help toolbar

**FIGURE A-16:** Create a document Help topic

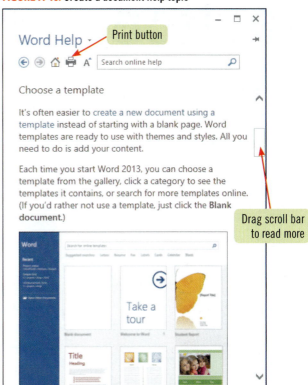

Print button

Drag scroll bar to read more

## Enabling touch mode

If you are using a touch screen with any of the Office 2013 apps, you can enable the touch mode to give the user interface a more spacious look. Enable touch mode by clicking the Quick Access toolbar list arrow, then clicking Touch/Mouse Mode to select it. Then you'll see the Touch Mode button in the Quick Access toolbar. Click , and you'll see the interface spread out.

## Recovering a document

Each Office program has a built-in recovery feature that allows you to open and save files that were open at the time of an interruption such as a power failure. When you restart the program(s) after an interruption, the Document Recovery task pane opens on the left side of your screen displaying both original and recovered versions of the files that were open. If you're not sure which file to open (original or recovered), it's usually better to open the recovered file because it will contain the latest information. You can, however, open and review all versions of the file that were recovered and save the best one. Each file listed in the Document Recovery task pane displays a list arrow with options that allow you to open the file, save it as is, delete it, or show repairs made to it during recovery.

# Practice

## Concepts Review

**Label the elements of the program window shown in** FIGURE A-17.

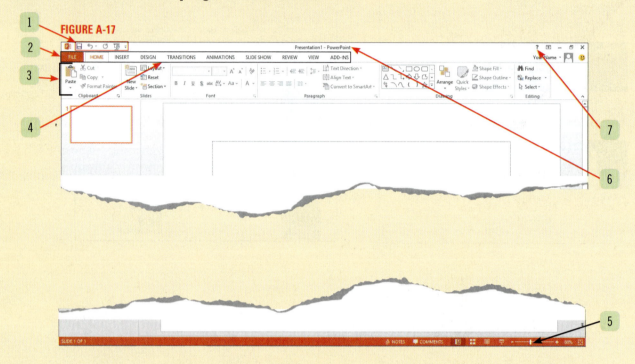

FIGURE A-17

## Match each project with the program for which it is best suited.

8. **Microsoft Access**
9. **Microsoft Excel**
10. **Microsoft Word**
11. **Microsoft PowerPoint**

a. Corporate convention budget with expense projections
b. Presentation for city council meeting
c. Business cover letter for a job application
d. Department store inventory

## Independent Challenge 1

You just accepted an administrative position with a local independently owned produce vendor that has recently invested in computers and is now considering purchasing Microsoft Office for the company. You are asked to propose ways Office might help the business. You produce your document in Word.

a. Start Word, create a new Blank document, then save the document as **OF A-Microsoft Office Document** in the location where you store your Data Files.
b. Change the zoom factor to 120%, type **Microsoft Word**, press [Enter] twice, type **Microsoft Excel**, press [Enter] twice, type **Microsoft PowerPoint**, press [Enter] twice, type **Microsoft Access**, press [Enter] twice, then type your name.
c. Click the line beneath each program name, type at least two tasks you can perform using that program (each separated by a comma), then press [Enter].
d. Save the document, then submit your work to your instructor as directed.
e. Exit Word.

# Getting Started with Excel 2013

**CASE** ▶ You have been hired as an assistant at Quest Specialty Travel (QST), a company offering tours that immerse travelers in regional culture. You report to Grace Wong, the vice president of finance. As Grace's assistant, you create worksheets to analyze data from various divisions of the company, so you can help her make sound decisions on company expansion and investments.

## Unit Objectives

After completing this unit, you will be able to:

- Understand spreadsheet software
- Identify Excel 2013 window components
- Understand formulas
- Enter labels and values and use the AutoSum button

- Edit cell entries
- Enter and edit a simple formula
- Switch worksheet views
- Choose print options

## Files You Will Need

EX A-1.xlsx
EX A-2.xlsx
EX A-3.xlsx
EX A-4.xlsx
EX A-5.xlsx

©Katerina Havelkova/Shutterstock

**Learning Outcomes**
- Describe the uses of Excel
- Define key spreadsheet terms

# Understand Spreadsheet Software

Microsoft Excel is the electronic spreadsheet program within the Microsoft Office suite. An **electronic spreadsheet** is an application you use to perform numeric calculations and to analyze and present numeric data. One advantage of a spreadsheet program over pencil and paper is that your calculations are updated automatically, so you can change entries without having to manually recalculate. **TABLE A-1** shows some of the common business tasks people accomplish using Excel. In Excel, the electronic spreadsheet you work in is called a **worksheet**, and it is contained in a file called a **workbook**, which has the file extension .xlsx. **CASE** > *At Quest Specialty Travel, you use Excel extensively to track finances and manage corporate data.*

## DETAILS

### When you use Excel, you have the ability to:

**QUICK TIP**

You can also use the **Quick Analysis tool** to easily create charts and other elements that help you visualize how data is distributed.

- **Enter data quickly and accurately**

  With Excel, you can enter information faster and more accurately than with pencil and paper. **FIGURE A-1** shows a payroll worksheet created using pencil and paper. **FIGURE A-2** shows the same worksheet created using Excel. Equations were added to calculate the hours and pay. You can use Excel to recreate this information for each week by copying the worksheet's structure and the information that doesn't change from week to week, then entering unique data and formulas for each week.

- **Recalculate data easily**

  Fixing typing errors or updating data is easy in Excel. In the payroll example, if you receive updated hours for an employee, you just enter the new hours and Excel recalculates the pay.

- **Perform what-if analysis**

  The ability to change data and quickly view the recalculated results gives you the power to make informed business decisions. For instance, if you're considering raising the hourly rate for an entry-level tour guide from $12.50 to $15.00, you can enter the new value in the worksheet and immediately see the impact on the overall payroll as well as on the individual employee. Any time you use a worksheet to ask the question "What if?" you are performing **what-if analysis**. Excel also includes a Scenario Manager where you can name and save different what-if versions of your worksheet.

- **Change the appearance of information**

  Excel provides powerful features, such as the Quick Analysis tool, for making information visually appealing and easier to understand. Format text and numbers in different fonts, colors, and styles to make it stand out.

- **Create charts**

  Excel makes it easy to create charts based on worksheet information. Charts are updated automatically in Excel whenever data changes. The worksheet in **FIGURE A-2** includes a 3-D pie chart.

- **Share information**

  It's easy for everyone at QST to collaborate in Excel using the company intranet, the Internet, or a network storage device. For example, you can complete the weekly payroll that your boss, Grace Wong, started creating. You can also take advantage of collaboration tools such as shared workbooks, so that multiple people can edit a workbook simultaneously.

**QUICK TIP**

The **flash fill** feature makes it easy to fill a range of text based on existing examples. Simply type [Ctrl][E] if Excel correctly matches the information you want and it will be entered in a cell for you.

- **Build on previous work**

  Instead of creating a new worksheet for every project, it's easy to modify an existing Excel worksheet. When you are ready to create next week's payroll, you can open the file for last week's payroll, save it with a new filename, and modify the information as necessary. You can also use predesigned, formatted files called **templates** to create new worksheets quickly. Excel comes with many templates that you can customize.

**FIGURE A-1:** Traditional paper worksheet

Quest Specialty Travel
Trip Advisor Division Payroll Calculator

| Name | Hours | O/T Hrs | Hrly Rate | Reg Pay | O/T Pay | Gross Pay |
|------|-------|---------|-----------|---------|---------|-----------|
| Brueghel, Pieter | 40 | 4 | 16.50 | 660– | 132– | 792– |
| Cortona, Livia | 35 | 0 | 11– | 385– | 0– | 385– |
| Klimt, Gustave | 40 | 2 | 13– | 520– | 52– | 572– |
| Le Pen, Jean-Marie | 29 | 0 | 15– | 435– | 0– | 435– |
| Martinez, Juan | 37 | 0 | 13– | 481– | 0– | 461– |
| Mioshi, Keiko | 39 | 0 | 20.50 | 799.50 | 0– | 799.50 |
| Sherwood, Burton | 40 | 0 | 16.50 | 660– | 0– | 660– |
| Strano, Riccardo | 40 | 8 | 16– | 640– | 256– | 896– |
| Wadsworth, Alicia | 40 | 5 | 13– | 520– | 130– | 650– |
| Yamamoto, Johji | 38 | 0 | 15– | 570– | 0– | 570– |

**FIGURE A-2:** Excel worksheet

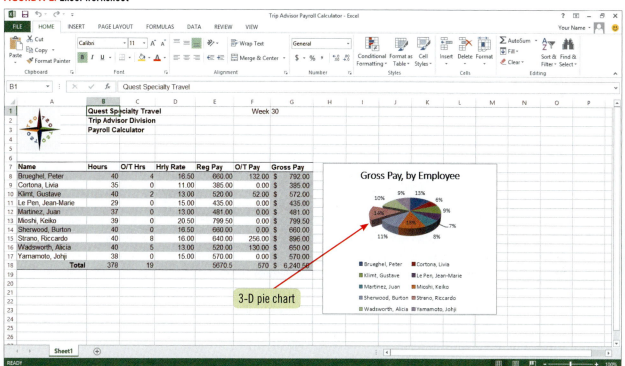

**TABLE A-1:** Business tasks you can accomplish using Excel

| you can use spreadsheets to | by |
|-----------------------------|----|
| Perform calculations | Adding formulas and functions to worksheet data; for example, adding a list of sales results or calculating a car payment |
| Represent values graphically | Creating charts based on worksheet data; for example, creating a chart that displays expenses |
| Generate reports | Creating workbooks that combine information from multiple worksheets, such as summarized sales information from multiple stores |
| Organize data | Sorting data in ascending or descending order; for example, alphabetizing a list of products or customer names, or prioritizing orders by date |
| Analyze data | Creating data summaries and short lists using PivotTables or AutoFilters; for example, making a list of the top 10 customers based on spending habits |
| Create what-if data scenarios | Using variable values to investigate and sample different outcomes, such as changing the interest rate or payment schedule on a loan |

# Identify Excel 2013 Window Components

**Learning Outcomes**
• Open and save an Excel file
• Identify Excel window elements

To start Excel, Microsoft Windows must be running. Similar to starting any program in Office, you can use the Start screen thumbnail on the Windows taskbar, the Start button on your keyboard, or you may have a shortcut on your desktop you prefer to use. If you need additional assistance, ask your instructor or technical support person. **CASE** ▶ *You decide to start Excel and familiarize yourself with the worksheet window.*

## STEPS

1. **Start Excel, click Open Other Workbooks on the navigation bar, click Computer, then click Browse to open the Open dialog box**

2. **In the Open dialog box, navigate to the location where you store your Data Files, click EX A-1.xlsx, click Open**

   The file opens in the Excel window.

3. **Click the FILE tab, click Save As on the navigation bar, click Computer, then click Browse to open the Save As dialog box**

4. **In the Save As dialog box, navigate to the location where you store your Data Files if necessary, type EX A-Trip Advisor Payroll Calculator in the File name text box, then click Save**

   Using **FIGURE A-3** as a guide, identify the following items:

   • The **Name box** displays the active cell address. "A1" appears in the Name box.
   • The **formula bar** allows you to enter or edit data in the worksheet.
   • The **worksheet window** contains a grid of columns and rows. Columns are labeled alphabetically and rows are labeled numerically. The worksheet window can contain a total of 1,048,576 rows and 16,384 columns. The intersection of a column and a row is called a **cell**. Cells can contain text, numbers, formulas, or a combination of all three. Every cell has its own unique location or **cell address**, which is identified by the coordinates of the intersecting column and row. The column and row indicators are shaded to make identifying the cell address easy.
   • The **cell pointer** is a dark rectangle that outlines the cell you are working in. This cell is called the **active cell**. In **FIGURE A-3**, the cell pointer outlines cell A1, so A1 is the active cell. The column and row headings for the active cell are highlighted, making it easier to locate.
   • **Sheet tabs** below the worksheet grid let you switch from sheet to sheet in a workbook. By default, a workbook file contains one worksheet—but you can have as many as 255, in a workbook. The New sheet button to the right of Sheet 1 allows you to add worksheets to a workbook. **Sheet tab scrolling buttons** let you navigate to additional sheet tabs when available.
   • You can use the **scroll bars** to move around in a worksheet that is too large to fit on the screen at once.
   • The **status bar** is located at the bottom of the Excel window. It provides a brief description of the active command or task in progress. **The mode indicator** in the lower-left corner of the status bar provides additional information about certain tasks.

5. **Click cell A4**

   Cell A4 becomes the active cell. To activate a different cell, you can click the cell or press the arrow keys on your keyboard to move to it.

6. **Click cell B5, press and hold the mouse button, drag ⬚ to cell B14, then release the mouse button**

   You selected a group of cells and they are highlighted, as shown in **FIGURE A-4**. A selection of two or more cells such as B5:B14 is called a **range**; you select a range when you want to perform an action on a group of cells at once, such as moving them or formatting them. When you select a range, the status bar displays the average, count (or number of items selected), and sum of the selected cells as a quick reference.

Getting Started with Excel 2013

**FIGURE A-3:** Open workbook

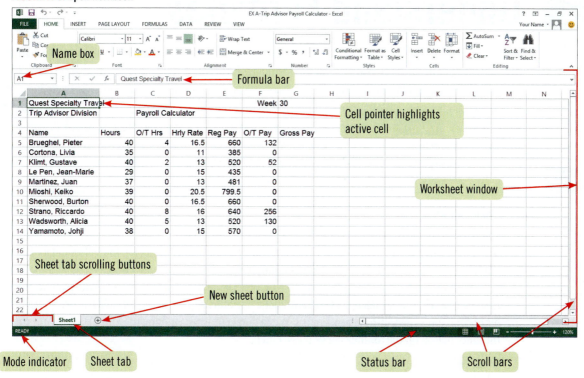

**FIGURE A-4:** Selected range

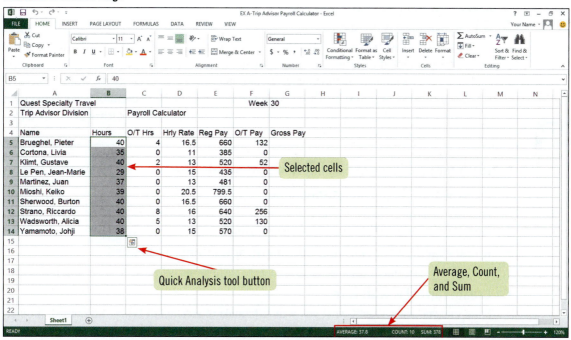

## Using SkyDrive and Web Apps

If you have a free Microsoft account, you can save your Excel files to SkyDrive, a free cloud-based service from Microsoft. When you save files to SkyDrive, you can access them on other devices–such as a tablet or smart phone. SkyDrive is available as an app on smart phones, which makes access very easy. You can open files to view them on any device and you can even make edits to them using **Office Web Apps**, which are simplified versions of the apps found in the Office 2013 suite. Because the Web Apps are online, they take up no computer disk space, and you can use them on any Internet-connected device. You can find more information in the "Working in the Cloud" appendix.

# Understand Formulas

**Learning Outcomes**
- Explain how a formula works
- Identify Excel arithmetic operators

Excel is a truly powerful program because users at every level of mathematical expertise can make calculations with accuracy. To do so, you use formulas. A **formula** is an equation in a worksheet. You use formulas to make calculations as simple as adding a column of numbers, or as complex as creating profit-and-loss projections for a global corporation. To tap into the power of Excel, you should understand how formulas work. **CASE** *Managers at QST use the Trip Advisor Payroll Calculator workbook to keep track of employee hours prior to submitting them to the Payroll Department. You'll be using this workbook regularly, so you need to understand the formulas it contains and how Excel calculates the results.*

## STEPS

1. **Click cell E5**

    The active cell contains a formula, which appears on the formula bar. All Excel formulas begin with the equal sign ( = ). If you want a cell to show the result of adding 4 plus 2, the formula in the cell would look like this: =4+2. If you want a cell to show the result of multiplying two values in your worksheet, such as the values in cells B5 and D5, the formula would look like this: =B5*D5, as shown in **FIGURE A-5**. While you're entering a formula in a cell, the cell references and arithmetic operators appear on the formula bar. See **TABLE A-2** for a list of commonly used arithmetic operators. When you're finished entering the formula, you can either click the Enter button on the formula bar or press [Enter].

2. **Click cell F5**

    An example of a more complex formula is the calculation of overtime pay. At QST, overtime pay is calculated at twice the regular hourly rate times the number of overtime hours. The formula used to calculate overtime pay for the employee in row 5 is:

    O/T Hrs times (2 times Hrly Rate)

    In the worksheet cell, you would enter: =C5*(2*D5), as shown in **FIGURE A-6**. The use of parentheses creates groups within the formula and indicates which calculations to complete first—an important consideration in complex formulas. In this formula, first the hourly rate is multiplied by 2, because that calculation is within the parentheses. Next, that value is multiplied by the number of overtime hours. Because overtime is calculated at twice the hourly rate, managers are aware that they need to closely watch this expense.

## DETAILS

**In creating calculations in Excel, it is important to:**

- **Know where the formulas should be**

    An Excel formula is created in the cell where the formula's results should appear. This means that the formula calculating Gross Pay for the employee in row 5 will be entered in cell G5.

- **Know exactly what cells and arithmetic operations are needed**

    Don't guess; make sure you know exactly what cells are involved before creating a formula.

- **Create formulas with care**

    Make sure you know exactly what you want a formula to accomplish before it is created. An inaccurate formula may have far-reaching effects if the formula or its results are referenced by other formulas, as shown in the payroll example in **FIGURE A-6**.

- **Use cell references rather than values**

    The beauty of Excel is that whenever you change a value in a cell, any formula containing a reference to that cell is automatically updated. For this reason, it's important that you use cell references in formulas, rather than actual values, whenever possible.

- **Determine what calculations will be needed**

    Sometimes it's difficult to predict what data will be needed within a worksheet, but you should try to anticipate what statistical information may be required. For example, if there are columns of numbers, chances are good that both column and row totals should be present.

Getting Started with Excel 2013

**FIGURE A-5:** Viewing a formula

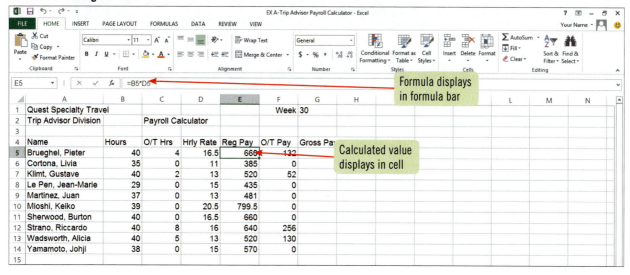

Formula displays in formula bar

Calculated value displays in cell

**FIGURE A-6:** Formula with multiple operators

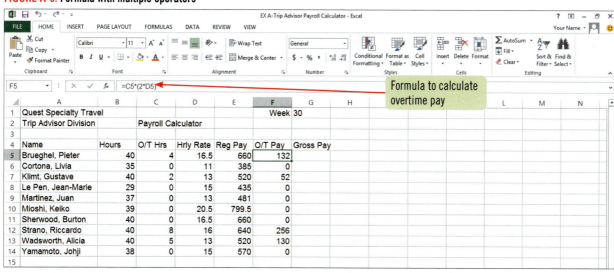

Formula to calculate overtime pay

**TABLE A-2:** Excel arithmetic operators

| operator | purpose | example |
|----------|---------|---------|
| + | Addition | =A5+A7 |
| - | Subtraction or negation | =A5-10 |
| * | Multiplication | =A5*A7 |
| / | Division | =A5/A7 |
| % | Percent | =35% |
| ^ (caret) | Exponent | =6^2 (same as $6^2$) |

# Enter Labels and Values and Use the AutoSum Button

To enter content in a cell, you can type in the formula bar or directly in the cell itself. When entering content in a worksheet, you should start by entering all the labels first. **Labels** are entries that contain text and numerical information not used in calculations, such as "2012 Sales" or "Travel Expenses". Labels help you identify data in worksheet rows and columns, making your worksheet easier to understand. **Values** are numbers, formulas, and functions that can be used in calculations. To enter a calculation, you type an equal sign (=) plus the formula for the calculation; some examples of an Excel calculation are "=2+2" and "=C5+C6". Functions are Excel's built-in formulas; you learn more about them in the next unit. **CASE** *You want to enter some information in the Trip Advisor Payroll Calculator workbook, and use a very simple function to total a range of cells.*

## STEPS

1. **Click cell A15, then click in the formula bar**

   Notice that the **mode indicator** on the status bar now reads "Edit," indicating you are in Edit mode. You are in Edit mode any time you are entering or changing the contents of a cell.

2. **Type Totals, then click the Enter button ✓ on the formula bar**

   Clicking the Enter button accepts the entry. The new text is left-aligned in the cell. Labels are left-aligned by default, and values are right-aligned by default. Excel recognizes an entry as a value if it is a number or it begins with one of these symbols: +, -, =, @, #, or $. When a cell contains both text and numbers, Excel recognizes it as a label.

3. **Click cell B15**

   You want this cell to total the hours worked by all the trip advisors. You might think you need to create a formula that looks like this: =B5+B6+B7+B8+B9+B10+B11+B12+B13+B14. However, there's an easier way to achieve this result.

4. **Click the AutoSum button Σ in the Editing group on the HOME tab on the Ribbon**

   The SUM function is inserted in the cell, and a suggested range appears in parentheses, as shown in **FIGURE A-7**. A **function** is a built-in formula; it includes the **arguments** (the information necessary to calculate an answer) as well as cell references and other unique information. Clicking the AutoSum button sums the adjacent range (that is, the cells next to the active cell) above or to the left, although you can adjust the range if necessary by selecting a different range before accepting the cell entry. Using the SUM function is quicker than entering a formula, and using the range B5:B14 is more efficient than entering individual cell references.

5. **Click ✓ on the formula bar**

   Excel calculates the total contained in cells B5:B14 and displays the result, 378, in cell B15. The cell actually contains the formula =SUM(B5:B14), and the result is displayed.

6. **Click cell C13, type 6, then press [Enter]**

   The number 6 replaces the cell's contents, the cell pointer moves to cell C14, and the value in cell F13 changes.

7. **Click cell C18, type Average Gross Pay, then press [Enter]**

   The new label is entered in cell C18. The contents appear to spill into the empty cells to the right.

8. **Click cell B15, position the pointer on the lower-right corner of the cell (the fill handle) so that the pointer changes to +, drag the + to cell G15, then release the mouse button**

   Dragging the fill handle across a range of cells copies the contents of the first cell into the other cells in the range. In the range B15:G15, each filled cell now contains a function that sums the range of cells above, as shown in **FIGURE A-8**.

9. **Save your work**

Getting Started with Excel 2013

**FIGURE A-7:** Creating a formula using the AutoSum button

**FIGURE A-7:** Creating a formula using the AutoSum button

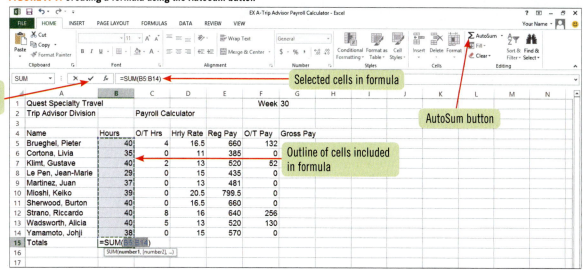

Enter button

Selected cells in formula

AutoSum button

Outline of cells included in formula

**FIGURE A-8:** Results of copied SUM functions

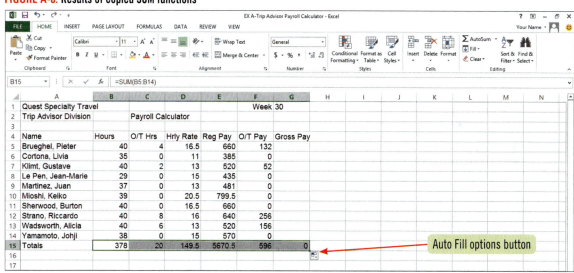

Auto Fill options button

## Navigating a worksheet

With over a million cells available in a worksheet, it is important to know how to move around in, or **navigate**, a worksheet. You can use the arrow keys on the keyboard ↑ , ↓ , → or ← to move one cell at a time, or press [Page Up] or [Page Down] to move one screen at a time. To move one screen to the left press [Alt][Page Up]; to move one screen to the right press

[Alt][Page Down]. You can also use the mouse pointer to click the desired cell. If the desired cell is not visible in the worksheet window, use the scroll bars or use the Go To command by clicking the Find & Select button in the Editing group on the HOME tab on the Ribbon. To quickly jump to the first cell in a worksheet press [Ctrl][Home]; to jump to the last cell, press [Ctrl][End].

# Edit Cell Entries

**Learning Outcomes**
• Edit cell entries in the formula bar
• Edit cell entries in the cell

You can change, or **edit**, the contents of an active cell at any time. To do so, double-click the cell, click in the formula bar, or just start typing. Excel switches to Edit mode when you are making cell entries. Different pointers, shown in **TABLE A-3**, guide you through the editing process. **CASE** *You noticed some errors in the worksheet and want to make corrections. The first error is in cell A5, which contains a misspelled name.*

## STEPS

1. **Click cell A5, then click to the right of P in the formula bar**

   As soon as you click in the formula bar, a blinking vertical line called the **insertion point** appears on the formula bar at the location where new text will be inserted. See **FIGURE A-9**. The mouse pointer changes to ⱂ when you point anywhere in the formula bar.

2. **Press [Delete], then click the Enter button ✓ on the formula bar**

   Clicking the Enter button accepts the edit, and the spelling of the employee's first name is corrected. You can also press [Enter] or [Tab] to accept an edit. Pressing [Enter] to accept an edit moves the cell pointer down one cell, and pressing [Tab] to accept an edit moves the cell pointer one cell to the right.

   > **QUICK TIP**
   > On some keyboards, you might need to press an [F Lock] key to enable the function keys.

3. **Click cell B6, then press [F2]**

   Excel switches to Edit mode, and the insertion point blinks in the cell. Pressing [F2] activates the cell for editing directly in the cell instead of the formula bar. Whether you edit in the cell or the formula bar is simply a matter of preference; the results in the worksheet are the same.

   > **QUICK TIP**
   > The Undo button allows you to reverse up to 100 previous actions, one at a time.

4. **Press [Backspace], type 8, then press [Enter]**

   The value in the cell changes from 35 to 38, and cell B7 becomes the active cell. Did you notice that the calculations in cells B15 and E15 also changed? That's because those cells contain formulas that include cell B6 in their calculations. If you make a mistake when editing, you can click the Cancel button ✗ on the formula bar *before* pressing [Enter] to confirm the cell entry. The Enter and Cancel buttons appear only when you're in Edit mode. If you notice the mistake *after* you have confirmed the cell entry, click the Undo button ↩ on the Quick Access toolbar.

   > **QUICK TIP**
   > You can use the keyboard to select all cell contents by clicking to the right of the cell contents in the cell or formula bar, pressing and holding [Shift], then pressing [Home].

5. **Click cell A9, then double-click the word Juan in the formula bar**

   Double-clicking a word in a cell selects it. When you selected the word, the Mini toolbar automatically displayed.

6. **Type Javier, then press [Enter]**

   When text is selected, typing deletes it and replaces it with the new text.

7. **Double-click cell C12, press [Delete], type 4, then click ✓**

   Double-clicking a cell activates it for editing directly in the cell. Compare your screen to **FIGURE A-10**.

8. **Save your work**

   Your changes to the workbook are saved.

---

### Recovering unsaved changes to a workbook file

You can use Excel's AutoRecover feature to automatically save (Autosave) your work as often as you want. This means that if you suddenly lose power or if Excel closes unexpectedly while you're working, you can recover all or some of the changes you made since you saved it last. (Of course, this is no substitute for regularly saving your work: this is just added insurance.) To customize the AutoRecover settings, click the FILE tab, click Options, then click Save. AutoRecover lets you decide how often and into which location it should Autosave files. When you restart Excel after losing power, a Document Recovery pane opens and provides access to the saved and Autosaved versions of the files that were open when Excel closed. You can also click the FILE tab, click Open on the navigation bar, then click any file in the Recent Workbooks list to open Autosaved workbooks.

**FIGURE A-9:** Worksheet in Edit mode

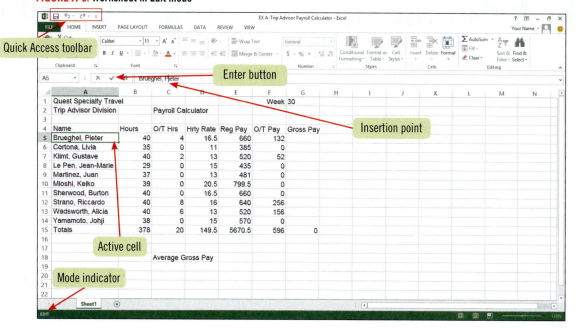

**FIGURE A-10:** Edited worksheet

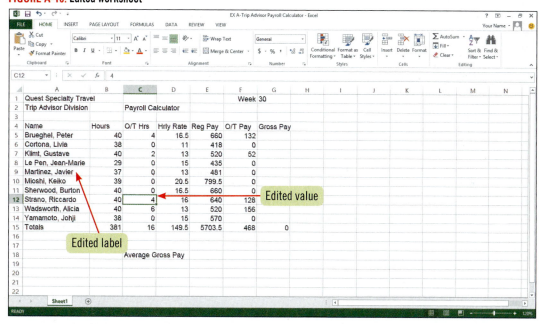

**TABLE A-3:** Common pointers in Excel

| name | pointer | use to | visible over the |
|---|---|---|---|
| Normal | | Select a cell or range; indicates Ready mode | Active worksheet |
| Fill handle | + | Copy cell contents to adjacent cells | Lower-right corner of the active cell or range |
| I-beam | I | Edit cell contents in active cell or formula bar | Active cell in Edit mode or over the formula bar |
| Move | | Change the location of the selected cell(s) | Perimeter of the active cell(s) |
| Copy | | Create a duplicate of the selected cell(s) | Perimeter of the active cell(s) when [Ctrl] is pressed |
| Column resize | | Change the width of a column | Border between column heading indicators |

Excel 2013

# Enter and Edit a Simple Formula

You use formulas in Excel to perform calculations such as adding, multiplying, and averaging. Formulas in an Excel worksheet start with the equal sign ( = ), also called the **formula prefix**, followed by cell addresses, range names, values, and **calculation operators**. Calculation operators indicate what type of calculation you want to perform on the cells, ranges, or values. They can include **arithmetic operators**, which perform mathematical calculations (see TABLE A-2 in the "Understand Formulas" lesson); **comparison operators**, which compare values for the purpose of true/false results; **text concatenation operators**, which join strings of text in different cells; and **reference operators**, which enable you to use ranges in calculations. **CASE** *You want to create a formula in the worksheet that calculates gross pay for each employee.*

## STEPS

1. **Click cell G5**

    This is the first cell where you want to insert the formula. To calculate gross pay, you need to add regular pay and overtime pay. For employee Peter Brueghel, regular pay appears in cell E5 and overtime pay appears in cell F5.

2. **Type =, click cell E5, type +, then click cell F5**

    Compare your formula bar to **FIGURE A-11**. The blue and red cell references in cell G5 correspond to the colored cell outlines. When entering a formula, it's a good idea to use cell references instead of values whenever you can. That way, if you later change a value in a cell (if, for example, Peter's regular pay changes to 690), any formula that includes this information reflects accurate, up-to-date results.

3. **Click the Enter button ☑ on the formula bar**

    The result of the formula =E5+F5, 792, appears in cell G5. This same value appears in cell G15 because cell G15 contains a formula that totals the values in cells G5:G14, and there are no other values at this time.

4. **Click cell F5**

    The formula in this cell calculates overtime pay by multiplying overtime hours (C5) times twice the regular hourly rate (2*D5). You want to edit this formula to reflect a new overtime pay rate.

5. **Click to the right of 2 in the formula bar, then type .5 as shown in FIGURE A-12**

    The formula that calculates overtime pay has been edited.

6. **Click ☑ on the formula bar**

    Compare your screen to **FIGURE A-13**. Notice that the calculated values in cells G5, F15, and G15 have all changed to reflect your edits to cell F5.

7. **Save your work**

---

### Understanding named ranges

It can be difficult to remember the cell locations of critical information in a worksheet, but using cell names can make this task much easier. You can name a single cell or range of contiguous, or touching, cells. For example, you might name a cell that contains data on average gross pay "AVG_GP" instead of trying to remember the cell address C18. A named range must begin with a letter or an underscore. It cannot contain any spaces or be the same as a built-in name, such as a function or another object (such as a different named range) in the workbook. To name a range, select the cell(s) you want to name, click the Name box in the formula bar, type the name you want to use, then press [Enter]. You can also name a range by clicking the FORMULAS tab, then clicking the Define Name button in the Defined Names group. Type the new range name in the Name text box in the New Name dialog box, verify the selected range, then click OK. When you use a named range in a formula, the named range appears instead of the cell address. You can also create a named range using the contents of a cell already in the range. Select the range containing the text you want to use as a name, then click the Create from Selection button in the Defined Names group. The Create Names from Selection dialog box opens. Choose the location of the name you want to use, then click OK.

**FIGURE A-11:** Simple formula in a worksheet

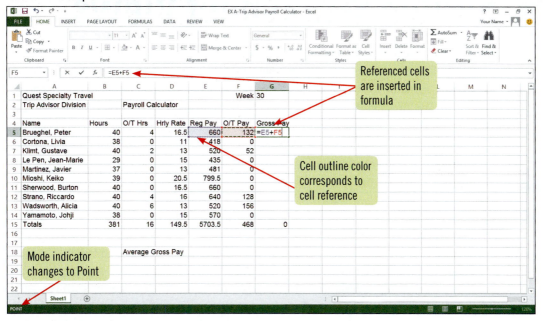

**FIGURE A-12:** Edited formula in a worksheet

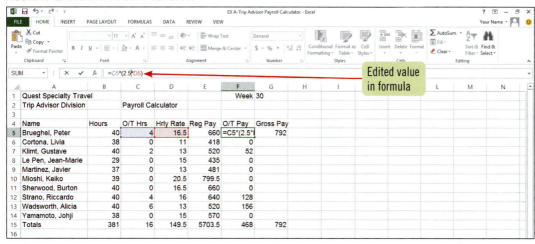

**FIGURE A-13:** Edited formula with changes

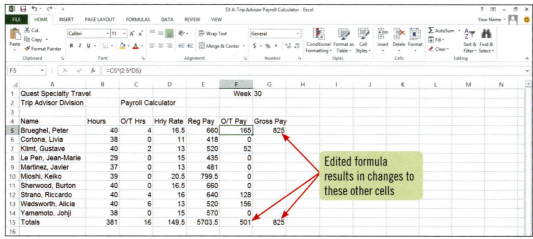

Excel 2013

# Switch Worksheet Views

**Learning Outcomes**
- Change worksheet views
- Create a header/footer
- Select a range

You can change your view of the worksheet window at any time, using either the VIEW tab on the Ribbon or the View buttons on the status bar. Changing your view does not affect the contents of a worksheet; it just makes it easier for you to focus on different tasks, such as entering content or preparing a worksheet for printing. The VIEW tab includes a variety of viewing options, such as View buttons, zoom controls, and the ability to show or hide worksheet elements such as gridlines. The status bar offers fewer View options but can be more convenient to use.  **CASE** ▶ *You want to make some final adjustments to your worksheet, including adding a header so the document looks more polished.*

## STEPS

**QUICK TIP**

Although a worksheet can contain more than a million rows and thousands of columns, the current document contains only as many pages as necessary for the current project.

1. **Click the VIEW tab on the Ribbon, then click the Page Layout button in the Workbook Views group**

   The view switches from the default view, Normal, to Page Layout view. **Normal view** shows the worksheet without including certain details like headers and footers, or tools like rulers and a page number indicator; it's great for creating and editing a worksheet, but may not be detailed enough when you want to put the finishing touches on a document. **Page Layout view** provides a more accurate view of how a worksheet will look when printed, as shown in **FIGURE A-14**. The margins of the page are displayed, along with a text box for the header. A footer text box appears at the bottom of the page, but your screen may not be large enough to view it without scrolling. Above and to the left of the page are rulers. Part of an additional page appears to the right of this page, but it is dimmed, indicating that it does not contain any data. A page number indicator on the status bar tells you the current page and the total number of pages in this worksheet.

2. **Move the pointer ⧉ over the header *without clicking***

   The header is made up of three text boxes: left, center, and right. Each text box is outlined in green as you pass over it with the pointer.

**QUICK TIP**

You can change header and footer information using the Header & Footer Tools Design tab that opens on the Ribbon when a header or footer is active. For example, you can insert the date by clicking the Current Date button in the Header & Footer Elements group, or insert the time by clicking the Current Time button.

3. **Click the left header text box, type Quest Specialty Travel, click the center header text box, type Trip Advisor Payroll Calculator, click the right header text box, then type Week 30**

   The new text appears in the text boxes, as shown in **FIGURE A-15**. You can also press the [Tab] key to advance from one header box to the next.

4. **Select the range A1:G2, then press [Delete]**

   The duplicate information you just entered in the header is deleted from cells in the worksheet.

5. **Click the VIEW tab if necessary, click the Ruler check box in the Show group, then click the Gridlines check box in the Show group**

   The rulers and the gridlines are hidden. By default, gridlines in a worksheet do not print, so hiding them gives you a more accurate image of your final document.

6. **Click the Page Break Preview button ▥ on the status bar**

   Your view changes to Page Break Preview, which displays a reduced view of each page of your worksheet, along with page break indicators that you can drag to include more or less information on a page.

7. **Drag the pointer ↕ from the bottom page break indicator to the bottom of row 20**

   See **FIGURE A-16**. When you're working on a large worksheet with multiple pages, sometimes you need to adjust where pages break; in this worksheet, however, the information all fits comfortably on one page.

**QUICK TIP**

Once you view a worksheet in Page Break Preview, the page break indicators appear as dotted lines after you switch back to Normal view or Page Layout view.

8. **Click the Page Layout button in the Workbook Views group, click the Ruler check box in the Show group, then click the Gridlines check box in the Show group**

   The rulers and gridlines are no longer hidden. You can show or hide VIEW tab items in any view.

9. **Save your work**

**FIGURE A-14:** Page Layout view

Turns ruler on/off

Workbook Views group

Turns gridlines on/off

Vertical ruler

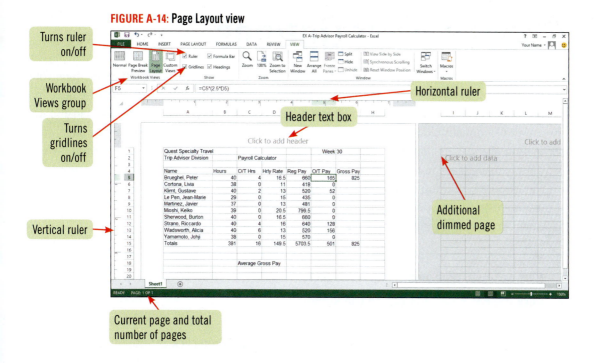

Horizontal ruler

Header text box

Additional dimmed page

Current page and total number of pages

**FIGURE A-15:** Header text entered

HEADER & FOOTER TOOLS tab

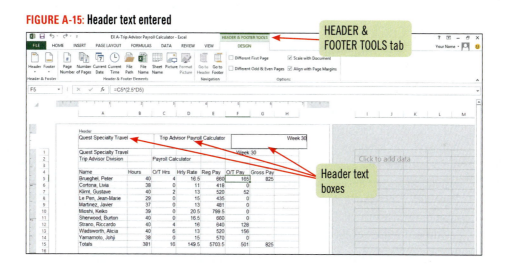

Header text boxes

**FIGURE A-16:** Page Break Preview

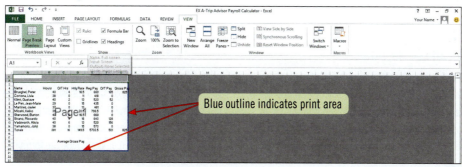

Blue outline indicates print area

# Choose Print Options

**Learning Outcomes**
- Change the page orientation
- Hide/view gridlines when printing
- Preview and print a worksheet

Before printing a document, you may want to review it using the PAGE LAYOUT tab to fine-tune your printed output. You can use tools on the PAGE LAYOUT tab to adjust print orientation (the direction in which the content prints across the page), paper size, and location of page breaks. You can also use the Scale to Fit options on the PAGE LAYOUT tab to fit a large amount of data on a single page without making changes to individual margins, and to turn gridlines and column/row headings on and off. When you are ready to print, you can set print options such as the number of copies to print and the correct printer, and you can preview your document in Backstage view using the FILE tab. You can also adjust page layout settings from within Backstage view and immediately see the results in the document preview. **CASE** *You are ready to prepare your worksheet for printing.*

## STEPS

1. **Click cell A20, type your name, then click ✓**

2. **Click the PAGE LAYOUT tab on the Ribbon**

   Compare your screen to **FIGURE A-17**. The solid outline indicates the default **print area**, the area to be printed.

**QUICK TIP**
You can use the Zoom slider on the status bar at any time to enlarge your view of specific areas of your worksheet.

3. **Click the Orientation button in the Page Setup group, then click Landscape**

   The paper orientation changes to **landscape**, so the contents will print across the length of the page instead of across the width.

4. **Click the Orientation button in the Page Setup group, then click Portrait**

   The orientation returns to **portrait**, so the contents will print across the width of the page.

5. **Click the Gridlines View check box in the Sheet Options group on the PAGE LAYOUT tab, click the Gridlines Print check box to select it if necessary, then save your work**

   Printing gridlines makes the data easier to read, but the gridlines will not print unless the Gridlines Print check box is checked.

**QUICK TIP**
To change the active printer, click the current printer in the Printer section in Backstage view, then choose a different printer.

6. **Click the FILE tab, then click Print on the navigation bar**

   The Print tab in Backstage view displays a preview of your worksheet exactly as it will look when it is printed. To the left of the worksheet preview, you can also change a number of document settings and print options. To open the Page Setup dialog box and adjust page layout options, click the Page Setup link in the Settings section. Compare your preview screen to **FIGURE A-18**. You can print from this view by clicking the Print button, or return to the worksheet without printing by clicking the Back button ⬅. You can also print an entire workbook from the Backstage view by clicking the Print button in the Settings section, then selecting the active sheet or entire workbook.

**QUICK TIP**
If the Quick Print button 🖨 appears on the Quick Access Toolbar, you can print your worksheet using the default settings by clicking it.

7. **Compare your settings to FIGURE A-18, then click the Print button**

   One copy of the worksheet prints.

8. **Submit your work to your instructor as directed, then exit Excel**

---

### Printing worksheet formulas

Sometimes you need to keep a record of all the formulas in a worksheet. You might want to do this to see exactly how you came up with a complex calculation, so you can explain it to others. To prepare a worksheet to show formulas rather than results when printed, open the workbook containing the formulas you want to print. Click the FORMULAS tab, then click the Show Formulas button in the Formula Auditing group to select it. When the Show Formulas button is selected, formulas rather than resulting values are displayed in the worksheet on screen and when printed. (The Show Formulas button is a *toggle*: click it again to hide the formulas.)

**FIGURE A-17:** Worksheet with Portrait orientation

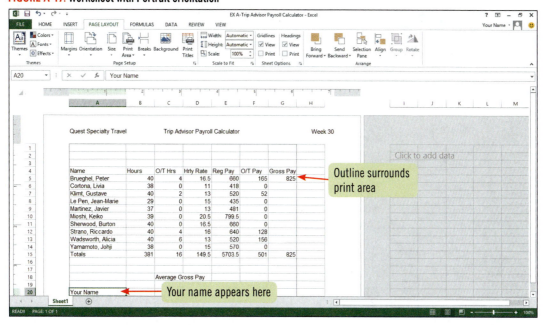

**FIGURE A-18:** Worksheet in Backstage view

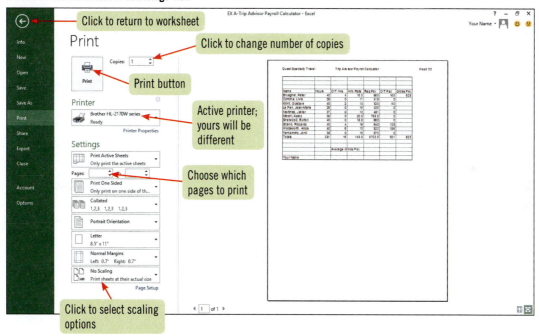

## Scaling to fit

If you have a large amount of data that you want to fit to a single sheet of paper, but you don't want to spend a lot of time trying to adjust the margins and other settings, you have several options. You can easily print your work on a single sheet by clicking the No Scaling list arrow in the Settings section on the Print button in Backstage view, then clicking Fit Sheet on One Page. Another method for fitting worksheet content onto one page is to click the PAGE LAYOUT tab, then change the Width and Height settings in the Scale to Fit group each to 1 Page. You can also use the Fit to option in the Page Setup dialog box to fit a worksheet on one page. To open the Page Setup dialog box, click the dialog box launcher in the Scale to Fit group on the PAGE LAYOUT tab, or click the Page Setup link on the Print tab in Backstage view. Make sure the Page tab is selected in the Page Setup dialog box, then click the Fit to option button.

# Practice

## Concepts Review

**Label the elements of the Excel worksheet window shown in** FIGURE A-19.

FIGURE A-19

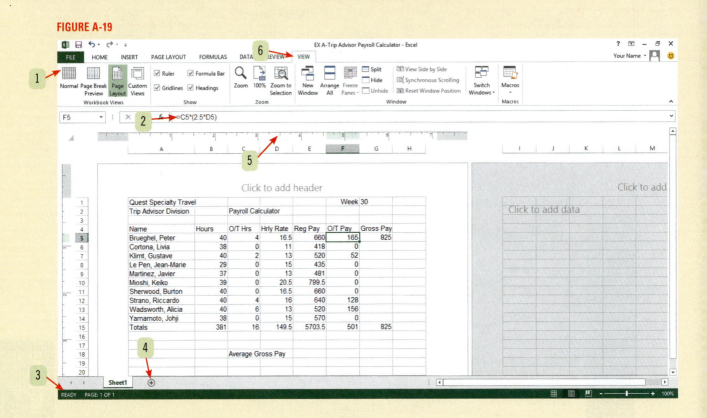

## Match each term with the statement that best describes it.

| | |
|---|---|
| 7. **Cell** | **a.** Part of the Excel program window that displays the active cell address |
| 8. **Orientation** | **b.** Default view in Excel |
| 9. **Normal view** | **c.** Direction in which contents of page will print |
| 10. **Formula prefix** | **d.** Equal sign preceding a formula |
| 11. **Workbook** | **e.** File consisting of one or more worksheets |
| 12. **Name box** | **f.** Intersection of a column and a row |

**Select the best answer from the list of choices.**

13. The maximum number of worksheets you can include in a workbook is:
    - **a.** 3.
    - **b.** 250.
    - **c.** 255.
    - **d.** Unlimited.

14. Which feature could be used to print a very long worksheet on a single sheet of paper?
    - **a.** Show Formulas
    - **b.** Scale to fit
    - **c.** Page Break Preview
    - **d.** Named Ranges

15. Using a cell address in a formula is known as:
    - **a.** Formularizing.
    - **b.** Prefixing.
    - **c.** Cell referencing.
    - **d.** Cell mathematics.

16. A selection of multiple cells is called a:
    - **a.** Group.
    - **b.** Range.
    - **c.** Reference.
    - **d.** Package.

17. In which area can you see a preview of your worksheet?
    - **a.** Page Setup
    - **b.** Backstage view
    - **c.** Printer Setup
    - **d.** VIEW tab

18. Which worksheet view shows how your worksheet will look when printed?
    - **a.** Page Layout
    - **b.** Data
    - **c.** Review
    - **d.** View

19. Which key can you press to switch to Edit mode?
    - **a.** [F1]
    - **b.** [F2]
    - **c.** [F4]
    - **d.** [F6]

20. In which view can you see the header and footer areas of a worksheet?
    - **a.** Normal view
    - **b.** Page Layout view
    - **c.** Page Break Preview
    - **d.** Header/Footer view

21. Which view shows you a reduced view of each page of your worksheet?
    - **a.** Normal
    - **b.** Page Layout
    - **c.** Thumbnail
    - **d.** Page Break Preview

## Skills Review

1. **Understand spreadsheet software.**
   - **a.** What is the difference between a workbook and a worksheet?
   - **b.** Identify five common business uses for electronic spreadsheets.
   - **c.** What is what-if analysis?

2. **Identify Excel 2013 window components.**
   - **a.** Start Excel.
   - **b.** Open the file EX A-2.xlsx from the location where you store your Data Files, then save it as **EX A-Weather Statistics**.
   - **c.** Locate the formula bar, the Sheet tabs, the mode indicator, and the cell pointer.

3. **Understand formulas.**
   - **a.** What is the average high temperature of the listed cities? (*Hint*: Select the range B5:G5 and use the status bar.)
   - **b.** What formula would you create to calculate the difference in altitude between Atlanta and Phoenix? Enter your answer (as an equation) in cell D13.

# Skills Review (continued)

**4. Enter labels and values and use the AutoSum button.**

   **a.** Click cell H8, then use the AutoSum button to calculate the total snowfall.

   **b.** Click cell H7, then use the AutoSum button to calculate the total rainfall.

   **c.** Save your changes to the file.

**5. Edit cell entries.**

   **a.** Use [F2] to correct the spelling of SanteFe in cell G3 (the correct spelling is Santa Fe).

   **b.** Click cell A17, then type your name.

   **c.** Save your changes.

**6. Enter and edit a simple formula.**

   **a.** Change the value 41 in cell C8 to **52**.

   **b.** Change the value 37 in cell D6 to **35.4**.

   **c.** Select cell J4, then use the fill handle to copy the formula in cell J4 to cells J5:J8.

   **d.** Save your changes.

**7. Switch worksheet views.**

   **a.** Click the VIEW tab on the Ribbon, then switch to Page Layout view.

   **b.** Add the header **Average Annual Weather Statistics** to the center header text box.

   **c.** Add your name to the right header box.

   **d.** Delete the contents of cell A17.

   **e.** Delete the contents of cell A1.

   **f.** Save your changes.

**8. Choose print options.**

   **a.** Use the PAGE LAYOUT tab to change the orientation to Portrait.

   **b.** Turn off gridlines by deselecting both the Gridlines View and Gridlines Print check boxes (if necessary) in the Sheet Options group.

   **c.** Scale the worksheet so all the information fits on one page. If necessary, scale the worksheet so all the information fits on one page. (*Hint*: Click the Width list arrow in the Scale to Fit group, click 1 page, click the Height list arrow in the Scale to Fit group, then click 1 page.) Compare your screen to **FIGURE A-20**.

   **d.** Preview the worksheet in Backstage view, then print the worksheet.

   **e.** Save your changes, submit your work to your instructor as directed, then close the workbook and exit Excel.

**FIGURE A-20**

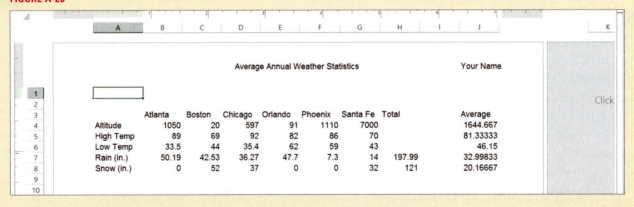

# Independent Challenge 1

A local executive relocation company has hired you to help them make the transition to using Excel in their office. They would like to list their properties in a workbook. You've started a worksheet for this project that contains labels but no data.

a. Open the file EX A-3.xlsx from the location where you store your Data Files, then save it as **EX A-Property Listings**.

b. Enter the data shown in **TABLE A-4** in columns A, C, D, and E (the property address information should spill into column B).

**TABLE A-4**

| Property Address | Price | Bedrooms | Bathrooms |
|---|---|---|---|
| 1507 Pinon Lane | 525000 | 4 | 2.5 |
| 32 Zanzibar Way | 325000 | 3 | 4 |
| 60 Pottery Lane | 475500 | 2 | 2 |
| 902 Excelsior Drive | 310000 | 4 | 3 |

© 2014 Cengage Learning

c. Use Page Layout view to create a header with the following components: the title **Property Listings** in the center and your name on the right.

d. Create formulas for totals in cells C6:E6.

e. Save your changes, then compare your worksheet to **FIGURE A-21**.

f. Submit your work to your instructor as directed.

g. Close the worksheet and exit Excel.

**FIGURE A-21**

# Independent Challenge 2

You are the General Manager for Prestige Import Motors, a small auto parts supplier. Although the company is just five years old, it is expanding rapidly, and you are continually looking for ways to save time. You recently began using Excel to manage and maintain data on inventory and sales, which has greatly helped you to track information accurately and efficiently.

a. Start Excel.

b. Save a new workbook as **EX A-Prestige Import Motors** in the location where you store your Data Files.

c. Switch to an appropriate view, then add a header that contains your name in the left header text box and the title **Prestige Import Motors** in the center header text box.

# Visual Workshop

Open the file EX A-5.xlsx from the location where you store your Data Files, then save it as **EX A-Inventory Items**. Using the skills you learned in this unit, modify your worksheet so it matches **FIGURE A-25**. Enter formulas in cells D4 through D13 and in cells B14 and C14. Use the AutoSum button and fill handle to make entering your formulas easier. Add your name in the left header text box, then print one copy of the worksheet with the formulas displayed.

**FIGURE A-25**

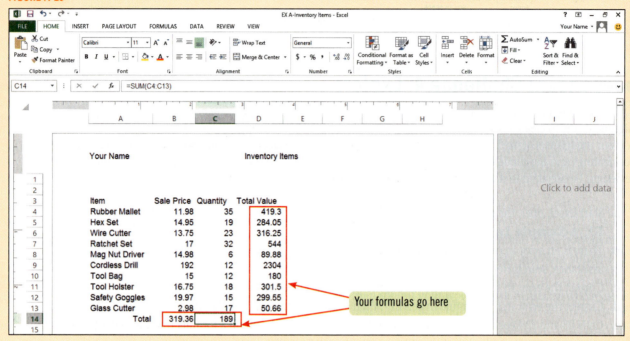

# Working with Formulas and Functions

**CASE**  Grace Wong, vice president of finance at Quest Specialty Travel, needs to analyze tour expenses for the current year. She has asked you to prepare a worksheet that summarizes this expense data and includes some statistical analysis. She would also like you to perform some what-if analysis, to see what quarterly expenses would look like with various projected increases.

## Unit Objectives

After completing this unit, you will be able to:

- Create a complex formula
- Insert a function
- Type a function
- Copy and move cell entries
- Understand relative and absolute cell references
- Copy formulas with relative cell references
- Copy formulas with absolute cell references
- Round a value with a function

## Files You Will Need

EX B-1.xlsx
EX B-2.xlsx
EX B-3.xlsx
EX B-4.xlsx

# Create a Complex Formula

A **complex formula** is one that uses more than one arithmetic operator. You might, for example, need to create a formula that uses addition and multiplication. In formulas containing more than one arithmetic operator, Excel uses the standard **order of precedence** rules to determine which operation to perform first. You can change the order of precedence in a formula by using parentheses around the part you want to calculate first. For example, the formula =4+2*5 equals 14, because the order of precedence dictates that multiplication is performed before addition. However, the formula =(4+2)*5 equals 30, because the parentheses cause 4+2 to be calculated first. **CASE** *You want to create a formula that calculates a 20% increase in tour expenses.*

## STEPS

1. **Start Excel, open the file EX B-1.xlsx from the location where you store your Data Files, then save it as EX B-Tour Expense Analysis**

2. **Select the range B4:B11, click the Quick Analysis tool ▦, then click the Totals tab**
   The Totals tab in the Quick Analysis tool displays commonly used functions, as seen in **FIGURE B-1**.

3. **Click the AutoSum button ▦ in the Quick Analysis tool**
   The newly calculated value displays in cell B12 and has a darker appearance than the figures in the selected range.

4. **Click cell B12, then drag the fill handle to cell E12**
   The formula in cell B12 is copied to cells C12:E12. The copied cells have the same dark appearance as that of cell B12.

5. **Click cell B14, type =, click cell B12, then type +**
   In this first part of the formula, you are using a reference to the total expenses for Quarter 1.

6. **Click cell B12, then type *.2**
   The second part of this formula adds a 20% increase (B12*.2) to the original value of the cell (the total expenses for Quarter 1).

7. **Click the Enter button ✓ on the formula bar**
   The result, 41789.556, appears in cell B14.

8. **Press [Tab], type =, click cell C12, type +, click cell C12, type *.2, then click ✓**
   The result, 41352.912, appears in cell C14.

9. **Drag the fill handle from cell C14 to cell E14**
   The calculated values appear in the selected range, as shown in **FIGURE B-2**. Dragging the fill handle on a cell copies the cell's contents or continues a series of data (such as Quarter 1, Quarter 2, etc.) into adjacent cells. This option is called **Auto Fill**.

10. **Save your work**

---

### Using Apps for Office to improve worksheet functionality

Excel has more functionality than simple and complex math computations. Using the Apps for Office feature (found in the Apps group in the INSERT tab), you can insert an app into your worksheet that accesses the web and adds functionality to your work. Many of the available apps are free and can be used to create an email, appointment, meeting, contact, or task, or be a reference source, such as the Mini Calendar and Date Picker. When you click the Apps for Office button, you'll see any Recently Used Apps. Click See All to display the featured apps and to go to the Office store to view available apps. When you find an app you want, make sure you're logged in to Office.com (you may need to log in again), click the app, click Add, then follow the prompts to download the app. Click the Apps for Office button, click See All, click the app you just added, then click Insert. The app will display as an embedded object in your worksheet and will also appear in the Recently Used Apps palette when you click the Apps for Office button.

**FIGURE B-1:** Totals tab in the Quick Analysis tool

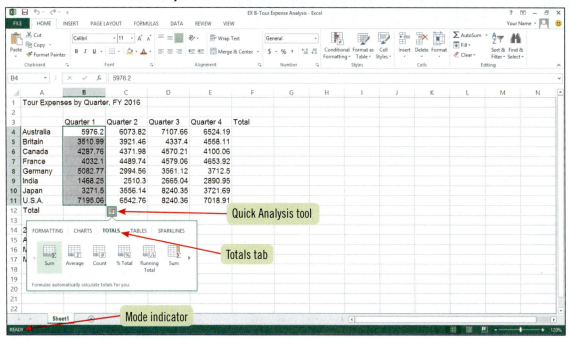

**FIGURE B-2:** Complex formulas in worksheet

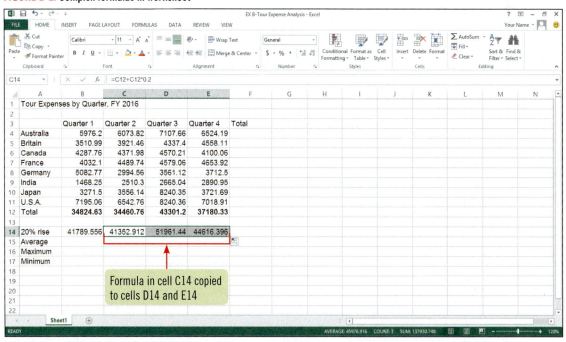

### Reviewing the order of precedence

When you work with formulas that contain more than one operator, the order of precedence is very important because it affects the final value. If a formula contains two or more operators, such as 4+.55/4000*25, Excel performs the calculations in a particular sequence based on the following rules: Operations inside parentheses are calculated before any other operations. Reference operators (such as ranges) are calculated first. Exponents are calculated next, then any multiplication and division—progressing from left to right. Finally, addition and subtraction are calculated from left to right. In the example 4+.55/4000*25, Excel performs the arithmetic operations by first dividing .55 by 4000, then multiplying the result by 25, then adding 4. You can change the order of calculations by using parentheses. For example, in the formula (4+.55)/4000*25, Excel would first add 4 and .55, then divide that amount by 4000, then finally multiply by 25.

Working with Formulas and Functions

# Insert a Function

**Learning Outcomes**
• Use the Insert Function button
• Select a range for use in a function
• Select a function from the AutoSum list arrow

**Functions** are predefined worksheet formulas that enable you to perform complex calculations easily. You can use the Insert Function button on the formula bar to choose a function from a dialog box. You can quickly insert the SUM function using the AutoSum button on the Ribbon, or you can click the AutoSum list arrow to enter other frequently used functions, such as AVERAGE. You can also use the Quick Analysis tool to calculate commonly used functions. Functions are organized into categories, such as Financial, Date & Time, and Statistical, based on their purposes. You can insert a function on its own or as part of another formula. For example, you have used the SUM function on its own to add a range of cells. You could also use the SUM function within a formula that adds a range of cells and then multiplies the total by a decimal. If you use a function alone, it always begins with an equal sign ( = ) as the formula prefix. **CASE** *You need to calculate the average expenses for the first quarter of the year, and decide to use a function to do so.*

## STEPS

1. **Click cell B15**

   This is the cell where you want to enter the calculation that averages expenses per country for the first quarter. You want to use the Insert Function dialog box to enter this function.

2. **Click the Insert Function button** $f_x$ **on the formula bar**

   An equal sign ( = ) is inserted in the active cell and in the formula bar, and the Insert Function dialog box opens, as shown in **FIGURE B-3**. In this dialog box, you specify the function you want to use by clicking it in the Select a function list. The Select a function list initially displays recently used functions. If you don't see the function you want, you can click the Or select a category list arrow to choose the desired category. If you're not sure which category to choose, you can type the function name or a description in the Search for a function field. The AVERAGE function is a statistical function, but you don't need to open the Statistical category because this function already appears in the Most Recently Used category.

3. **Click AVERAGE in the Select a function list if necessary, read the information that appears under the list, then click OK**

   The Function Arguments dialog box opens, in which you define the range of cells you want to average.

4. **Click the Collapse button** 🔲 **in the Number1 field of the Function Arguments dialog box, select the range B4:B11 in the worksheet, then click the Expand button** 🔲 **in the Function Arguments dialog box**

   Clicking the Collapse button minimizes the dialog box so you can select cells in the worksheet. When you click the Expand button, the dialog box is restored, as shown in **FIGURE B-4**. You can also begin dragging in the worksheet to automatically minimize the dialog box; after you select the desired range, the dialog box is restored.

5. **Click OK**

   The Function Arguments dialog box closes, and the calculated value is displayed in cell B15. The average expenses per country for Quarter 1 is 4353.0788.

6. **Click cell C15, click the AutoSum list arrow** $\Sigma$ **in the Editing group on the HOME tab, then click Average**

   A ScreenTip beneath cell C15 displays the arguments needed to complete the function. The text "number1" is shown in boldface type, telling you that the next step is to supply the first cell in the group you want to average. You want to average a range of cells.

7. **Select the range C4:C11 in the worksheet, then click the Enter button** ✓ **on the formula bar**

   The average expenses per country for the second quarter appears in cell C15.

8. **Drag the fill handle from cell C15 to cell E15**

   The formula in cell C15 is copied to the rest of the selected range, as shown in **FIGURE B-5**.

9. **Save your work**

Working with Formulas and Functions

**FIGURE B-3:** Insert Function dialog box

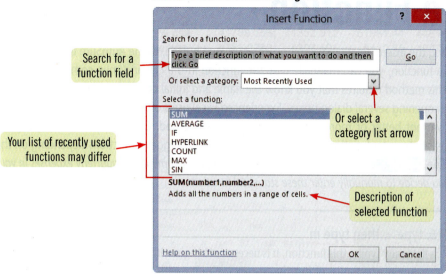

Search for a function field →

Your list of recently used functions may differ →

Or select a category list arrow

Description of selected function

**FIGURE B-4:** Expanded Function Arguments dialog box

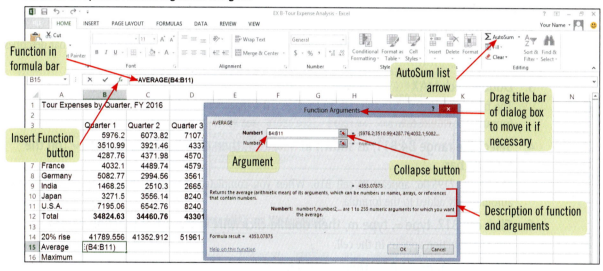

Function in formula bar

Insert Function button

AutoSum list arrow

Drag title bar of dialog box to move it if necessary

Argument

Collapse button

Description of function and arguments

**FIGURE B-5:** Average functions used in worksheet

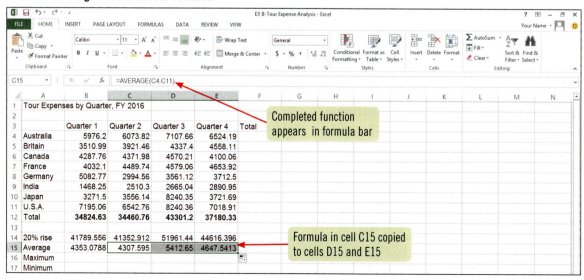

Completed function appears in formula bar

Formula in cell C15 copied to cells D15 and E15

# Copy and Move Cell Entries

**Learning Outcomes**
- Copy a range to the Clipboard
- Paste a Clipboard entry
- Empty cell contents
- Copy cell contents

There are three ways you can copy or move cells and ranges (or the contents within them) from one location to another: the Cut, Copy, and Paste buttons on the HOME tab on the Ribbon; the fill handle in the lower-right corner of the active cell or range; or the drag-and-drop feature. When you copy cells, the original data remains in the original location; when you cut or move cells, the original data is deleted from its original location. You can also cut, copy, and paste cells or ranges from one worksheet to another. **CASE** ➤ *In addition to the 20% rise in tour expenses, you also want to show a 30% rise. Rather than retype this information, you copy and move the labels in these cells.*

## STEPS

1. **Select the range B3:E3, then click the Copy button ▤ in the Clipboard group on the HOME tab**

   The selected range (B3:E3) is copied to the **Clipboard**, a temporary Windows storage area that holds the selections you copy or cut. A moving border surrounds the selected range until you press [Esc] or copy an additional item to the Clipboard.

2. **Click the dialog box launcher ▣ in the Clipboard group**

   The Office Clipboard opens in the Clipboard task pane, as shown in FIGURE B-9. When you copy or cut an item, it is cut or copied both to the Clipboard provided by Windows and to the Office Clipboard. Unlike the Windows Clipboard, which holds just one item at a time, the Office Clipboard contains up to 24 of the most recently cut or copied items from any Office program. Your Clipboard task pane may contain more items than shown in the figure.

3. **Click cell B19, then click the Paste button in the Clipboard group**

   A copy of the contents of range B3:E3 is pasted into the range B19:E19. When pasting an item from the Office Clipboard or Clipboard into a worksheet, you only need to specify the upper-left cell of the range where you want to paste the selection. Notice that the information you copied remains in the original range B3:E3; if you had cut instead of copied, the information would have been deleted from its original location once it was pasted.

4. **Press [Delete]**

   The selected cells are empty. You have decided to paste the cells in a different row. You can repeatedly paste an item from the Office Clipboard as many times as you like, as long as the item remains in the Office Clipboard.

5. **Click cell B20, click the first item in the Office Clipboard, then click the Close button ☒ on the Clipboard task pane**

   Cells B20:E20 contain the copied labels.

6. **Click cell A14, press and hold [Ctrl], point to any edge of the cell until the pointer changes to ⇦, drag cell A14 to cell A21, release the mouse button, then release [Ctrl]**

   The copy pointer ⇧ continues to appear as you drag, as shown in FIGURE B-10. When you release the mouse button, the contents of cell A14 are copied to cell A21.

7. **Click to the right of 2 in the formula bar, press [Backspace], type 3, then press [Enter]**

8. **Click cell B21, type =, click cell B12, type *1.3, click the Enter button ✓ on the formula bar, then save your work**

   This new formula calculates a 30% increase of the expenses for Quarter 1, though using a different method from what you previously used. Anything you multiply by 1.3 returns an amount that is 130% of the original amount, or a 30% increase. Compare your screen to FIGURE B-11.

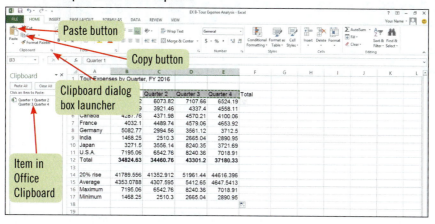

**FIGURE B-9:** Copied data in Office Clipboard

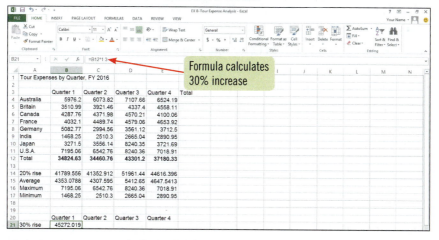

**FIGURE B-10:** Copying cell contents with drag-and-drop

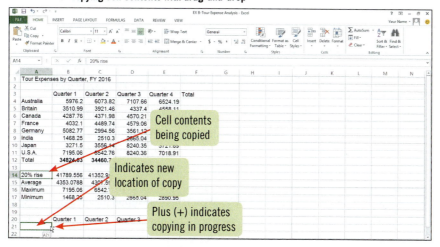

**FIGURE B-11:** Formula entered to calculate a 30% increase

## Inserting and deleting selected cells

As you add formulas to your workbook, you may need to insert or delete cells. When you do this, Excel automatically adjusts cell references to reflect their new locations. To insert cells, click the Insert list arrow in the Cells group on the HOME tab, then click Insert Cells. The Insert dialog box opens, asking if you want to insert a cell and move the current active cell down or to the right of the new one. To delete one or more selected cells, click the Delete list arrow in the Cells group, click Delete Cells, and in the Delete dialog box, indicate which way you want to move the adjacent cells. When using this option, be careful not to disturb row or column alignment that may be necessary to maintain the accuracy of cell references in the worksheet. Click the Insert button or Delete button in the Cells group to insert or delete a single cell.

**Learning Outcomes**
• Identify cell referencing
• Identify when to use absolute or relative cell references

# Understand Relative and Absolute Cell References

As you work in Excel, you may want to reuse formulas in different parts of a worksheet to reduce the amount of data you have to retype. For example, you might want to include a what-if analysis in one part of a worksheet showing a set of sales projections if sales increase by 10%. To include another analysis in another part of the worksheet showing projections if sales increase by 50%, you can copy the formulas from one section to another and simply change the "1" to a "5". But when you copy formulas, it is important to make sure that they refer to the correct cells. To do this, you need to understand the difference between relative and absolute cell references. **CASE** ➤ *You plan to reuse formulas in different parts of your worksheets, so you want to understand relative and absolute cell references.*

## DETAILS

### Consider the following when using relative and absolute cell references:

• **Use relative references when you want to preserve the relationship to the formula location**

When you create a formula that references another cell, Excel normally does not "record" the exact cell address for the cell being referenced in the formula. Instead, it looks at the relationship that cell has to the cell containing the formula. For example, in **FIGURE B-12**, cell F5 contains the formula: =SUM(B5:E5). When Excel retrieves values to calculate the formula in cell F5, it actually looks for "the four cells to the left of the formula," which in this case is cells B5:E5. This way, if you copy the cell to a new location, such as cell F6, the results will reflect the new formula location, and will automatically retrieve the values in cells B6, C6, D6, and E6. These are **relative cell references**, because Excel is recording the input cells *in relation to* or *relative to* the formula cell.

In most cases, you want to use relative cell references when copying or moving, so this is the Excel default. In **FIGURE B-12**, the formulas in F5:F12 and in B13:F13 contain relative cell references. They total the "four cells to the left of" or the "eight cells above" the formulas.

• **Use absolute cell references when you want to preserve the exact cell address in a formula**

There are times when you want Excel to retrieve formula information from a specific cell, and you don't want the cell address in the formula to change when you copy it to a new location. For example, you might have a price in a specific cell that you want to use in all formulas, regardless of their location. If you use relative cell referencing, the formula results would be incorrect, because Excel would use a different cell every time you copy the formula. Therefore you need to use an **absolute cell reference**, which is a reference that does not change when you copy the formula.

You create an absolute cell reference by placing a $ (dollar sign) in front of both the column letter and the row number of the cell address. You can either type the dollar sign when typing the cell address in a formula (for example, "=C12*$B$16"), or you can select a cell address on the formula bar and then press [F4] and the dollar signs are added automatically. **FIGURE B-13** shows formulas containing both absolute and relative references. The formulas in cells B19 to E26 use absolute cell references to refer to a potential sales increase of 50%, shown in cell B16.

**FIGURE B-12:** Formulas containing relative references

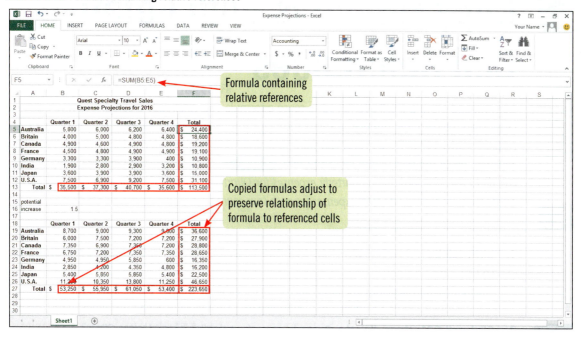

Formula containing relative references

Copied formulas adjust to preserve relationship of formula to referenced cells

**FIGURE B-13:** Formulas containing absolute and relative references

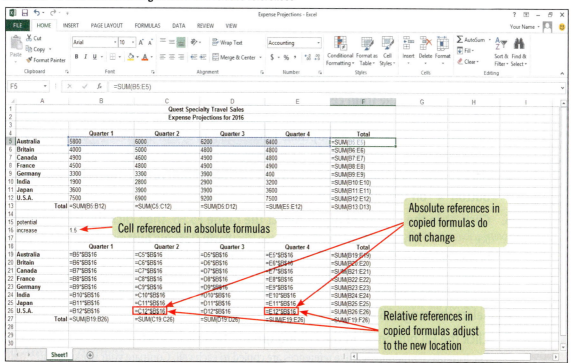

Absolute references in copied formulas do not change

Cell referenced in absolute formulas

Relative references in copied formulas adjust to the new location

## Using a mixed reference

Sometimes when you copy a formula, you want to change the row reference, but keep the column reference the same. This type of cell referencing combines elements of both absolute and relative referencing and is called a **mixed reference**. For example, when copied, a formula containing the mixed reference C$14 would change the column letter relative to its new location, but not the row number. In the mixed reference $C14, the

column letter would not change, but the row number would be updated relative to its location. Like an absolute reference, a mixed reference can be created by pressing the [F4] function key with the cell reference selected. With each press of the [F4] key, you cycle through all the possible combinations of relative, absolute, and mixed references (C14, $C$14, C$14, and $C14).

# Round a Value with a Function

The more you explore features and tools in Excel, the more ways you'll find to simplify your work and convey information more efficiently. For example, cells containing financial data are often easier to read if they contain fewer decimal places than those that appear by default. You can round a value or formula result to a specific number of decimal places by using the ROUND function. **CASE** ▶ *In your worksheet, you'd like to round the cells showing the 20% rise in expenses to show fewer digits; after all, it's not important to show cents in the projections, only whole dollars. You want Excel to round the calculated value to the nearest integer. You decide to edit cell B14 so it includes the ROUND function, and then copy the edited formula into the other formulas in this row.*

## STEPS

1. **Click cell B14, then click to the right of = in the formula bar**

   You want to position the function at the beginning of the formula, before any values or arguments.

2. **Type RO**

   Formula AutoComplete displays a list of functions beginning with RO beneath the formula bar.

3. **Double-click ROUND in the functions list**

   The new function and an opening parenthesis are added to the formula, as shown in **FIGURE B-19**. A few additional modifications are needed to complete your edit of the formula. You need to indicate the number of decimal places to which the function should round numbers and you also need to add a closing parenthesis around the set of arguments that comes after the ROUND function.

4. **Press [END], type ,0), then click the Enter button ✓ on the formula bar**

   The comma separates the arguments within the formula, and 0 indicates that you don't want any decimal places to appear in the calculated value. When you complete the edit, the parentheses at either end of the formula briefly become bold, indicating that the formula has the correct number of open and closed parentheses and is balanced.

5. **Drag the fill handle from cell B14 to cell E14**

   The formula in cell B14 is copied to the range C14:E14. All the values are rounded to display no decimal places. Compare your worksheet to **FIGURE B-20**.

6. **Scroll down so row 25 is visible, click cell A25, type your name, then click ✓ on the formula bar**

7. **Save your work, preview the worksheet in Backstage view, then submit your work to your Instructor as directed**

8. **Exit Excel**

**FIGURE B-19:** ROUND function added to an existing formula

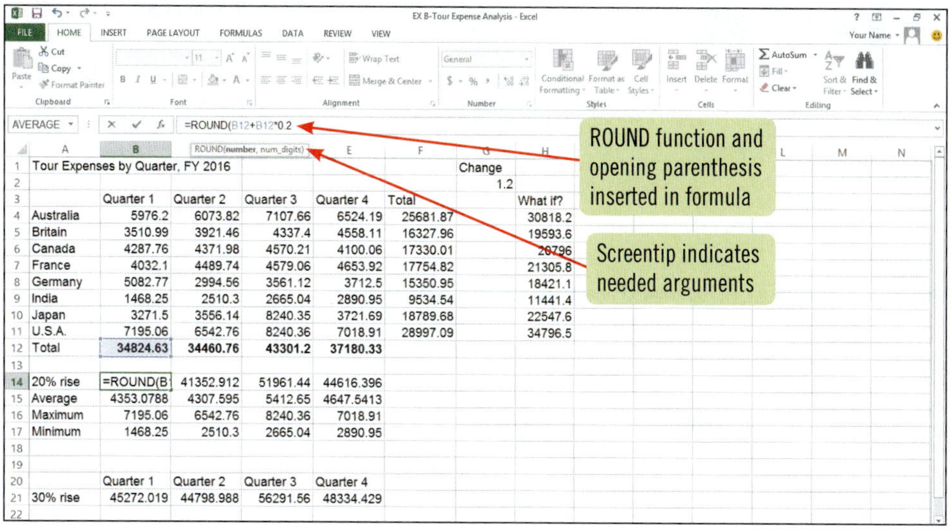

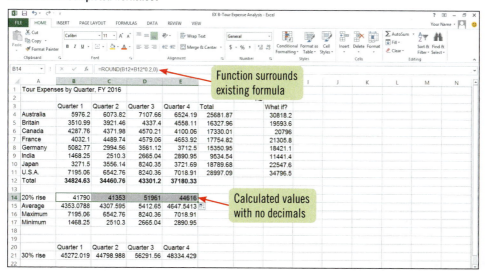

ROUND function and opening parenthesis inserted in formula

Screentip indicates needed arguments

**FIGURE B-20:** Completed worksheet

Function surrounds existing formula

Calculated values with no decimals

## Creating a new workbook using a template

Excel **templates** are predesigned workbook files intended to save time when you create common documents such as balance sheets, budgets, or time cards. Templates contain labels, values, formulas, and formatting, so all you have to do is customize them with your own information. Excel comes with many templates, and you can also create your own or find additional templates on the Web. Unlike a typical workbook, which has the file extension .xlsx, a template has the extension .xltx. To create a workbook using a template, click the FILE tab, then click New on the navigation bar. The New pane in Backstage view lists templates available through Office.com. The Blank workbook template is selected by default and is used to create a blank workbook with no content or special formatting. A preview of the selected template appears in a separate window on top of the New pane. To select a template, click one of the selections in the New pane, then click Create. **FIGURE B-21** shows an Office.com template. (Your list of templates may differ.) When you click Create, a new

workbook is created based on the template; when you save the new file in the default format, it has the regular .xlsx extension. To save a workbook of your own as a template, open the Save As dialog box, click the Save as type list arrow, then change the file type to Excel Template.

**FIGURE B-21:** EXPENSE TRENDS template selected in Backstage view

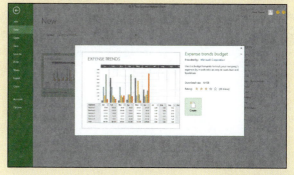

# Practice

## Concepts Review

Label each element of the Excel worksheet window shown in FIGURE B-22.

**FIGURE B-22**

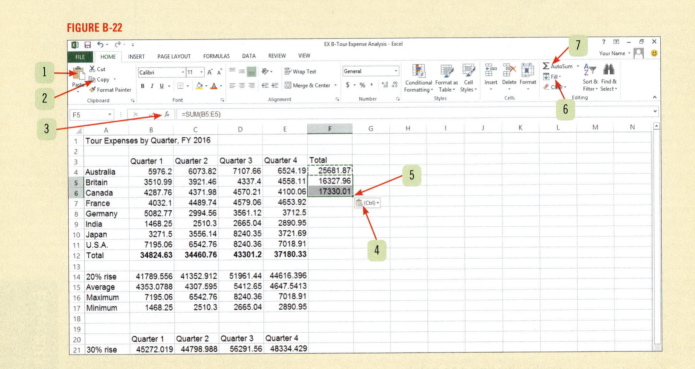

Match each term or button with the statement that best describes it.

8. **Fill handle**
9. **[Delete]**
10. **Dialog box launcher**
11. **Formula AutoComplete**
12. **Drag-and-drop method**

a. Clears the contents of selected cells

b. Item on the Ribbon that opens a dialog box or task pane

c. Lets you move or copy data from one cell to another without using the Clipboard

d. Displays an alphabetical list of functions from which you can choose

e. Lets you copy cell contents or continue a series of data into a range of selected cells

## Select the best answer from the list of choices.

**13. What type of cell reference changes when it is copied?**
   **a.** Circular
   **b.** Absolute
   **c.** Relative
   **d.** Specified

**14. What type of cell reference is C$19?**
   **a.** Relative
   **b.** Absolute
   **c.** Mixed
   **d.** Certain

**15. Which key do you press to copy while dragging and dropping selected cells?**
   **a.** [Alt]
   **b.** [Ctrl]
   **c.** [F2]
   **d.** [Tab]

**16. You can use any of the following features to enter a function *except*:**
   **a.** Insert Function button.
   **b.** Formula AutoComplete.
   **c.** AutoSum list arrow.
   **d.** Clipboard.

**17. Which key do you press to convert a relative cell reference to an absolute cell reference?**
   **a.** [F2]
   **b.** [F4]
   **c.** [F5]
   **d.** [F6]

# Skills Review

**1. Create a complex formula.**
   **a.** Open the file EX B-2.xlsx from the location where you store your Data Files, then save it as **EX B-Baking Supply Company Inventory**.
   **b.** Select the range B4:B8, click the Totals tab in the Quick Analysis tool, then click the AutoSum button.
   **c.** Use the fill handle to copy the formula in cell B9 to cells C9:E9
   **d.** In cell B11, create a complex formula that calculates a 30% decrease in the total number of cases of cake pans.
   **e.** Use the fill handle to copy this formula into cell C11 through cell E11.
   **f.** Save your work.

**2. Insert a function.**
   **a.** Use the AutoSum list arrow to create a formula in cell B13 that averages the number of cases of cake pans in each storage area.
   **b.** Use the Insert Function button to create a formula in cell B14 that calculates the maximum number of cases of cake pans in a storage area.
   **c.** Use the AutoSum list arrow to create a formula in cell B15 that calculates the minimum number of cases of cake pans in a storage area.
   **d.** Save your work.

**3. Type a function.**
   **a.** In cell C13, type a formula that includes a function to average the number of cases of pie pans in each storage area. (*Hint*: Use Formula AutoComplete to enter the function.)
   **b.** In cell C14, type a formula that includes a function to calculate the maximum number of cases of pie pans in a storage area.
   **c.** In cell C15, type a formula that includes a function to calculate the minimum number of cases of pie pans in a storage area.
   **d.** Save your work.

# Skills Review (continued)

4. **Copy and move cell entries.**
   a. Select the range B3:F3.
   b. Copy the selection to the Clipboard.
   c. Open the Clipboard task pane, then paste the selection into cell B17.
   d. Close the Clipboard task pane, then select the range A4:A9.
   e. Use the drag-and-drop method to copy the selection to cell A18. (*Hint*: The results should fill the range A18:A23.)
   f. Save your work.

5. **Understand relative and absolute cell references.**
   a. Write a brief description of the difference between relative and absolute references.
   b. List at least three situations in which you think a business might use an absolute reference in its calculations. Examples can include calculations for different types of worksheets, such as time cards, invoices, and budgets.

6. **Copy formulas with relative cell references.**
   a. Calculate the total in cell F4.
   b. Use the Fill button to copy the formula in cell F4 down to cells F5:F8.
   c. Select the range C13:C15.
   d. Use the fill handle to copy these cells to the range D13:F15.
   e. Save your work.

7. **Copy formulas with absolute cell references.**
   a. In cell H1, enter the value **1.575**.
   b. In cell H4, create a formula that multiplies F4 and an absolute reference to cell H1.
   c. Use the fill handle to copy the formula in cell H4 to cells H5 and H6.
   d. Use the Copy and Paste buttons to copy the formula in cell H4 to cells H7 and H8.
   e. Change the amount in cell H1 to **2.5**.
   f. Save your work.

8. **Round a value with a function.**
   a. Click cell H4.
   b. Edit this formula to include the ROUND function showing zero decimal places.
   c. Use the fill handle to copy the formula in cell H4 to the range H5:H8.
   d. Enter your name in cell A25, then compare your work to **FIGURE B-23**.
   e. Save your work, preview the worksheet in Backstage view, then submit your work to your instructor as directed.
   f. Close the workbook, then exit Excel.

**FIGURE B-23**

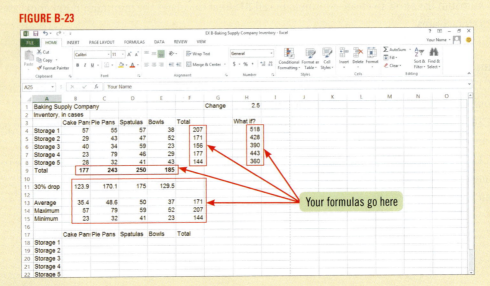

# Independent Challenge 1

You are thinking of starting a small express oil change service center. Before you begin, you need to evaluate what you think your monthly expenses will be. You've started a workbook, but need to complete the entries and add formulas.

a. Open the file EX B-3.xlsx from the location where you store your Data Files, then save it as **EX B-Express Oil Change Expenses**.

b. Make up your own expense data, and enter it in cells B4:B10. (Monthly sales are already included in the worksheet.)

c. Create a formula in cell C4 that calculates the annual rent.

d. Copy the formula in cell C4 to the range C5:C10.

e. Move the label in cell A15 to cell A14.

f. Create formulas in cells B11 and C11 that total the monthly and annual expenses.

g. Create a formula in cell C13 that calculates annual sales.

h. Create a formula in cell B14 that determines whether you will make a profit or loss, then copy the formula into cell C14.

i. Copy the labels in cells B3:C3 to cells E3:F3.

j. Type **Projected Increase** in cell G1, then type **.2** in cell H2.

k. Create a formula in cell E4 that calculates an increase in the monthly rent by the amount in cell H2. You will be copying this formula to other cells, so you'll need to use an absolute reference.

l. Create a formula in cell F4 that calculates the increased annual rent expense based on the calculation in cell E4.

m. Copy the formulas in cells E4:F4 into cells E5:F10 to calculate the remaining monthly and annual expenses.

n. Create a formula in cell E11 that calculates the total monthly expenses, then copy that formula to cell F11.

o. Copy the contents of cells B13:C13 into cells E13:F13.

p. Create formulas in cells E14 and F14 that calculate profit/loss based on the projected increase in monthly and annual expenses.

q. Change the projected increase to **.17**, then compare your work to the sample in **FIGURE B-24**.

r. Enter your name in a cell in the worksheet.

s. Save your work, preview the worksheet in Backstage view, submit your work to your instructor as directed, close the workbook, and exit Excel.

**FIGURE B-24**

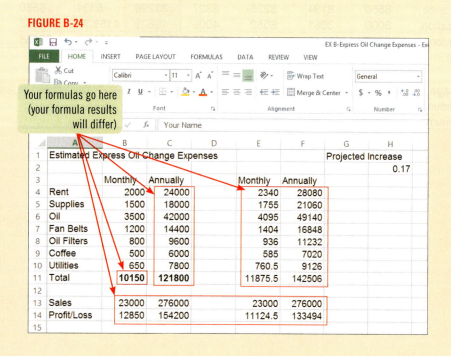

# Visual Workshop

Create the worksheet shown in **FIGURE B-28** using the skills you learned in this unit. Save the workbook as **EX B-Expense Analysis** to the location where you store your Data Files. Enter your name and worksheet title in the header as shown, hide the gridlines, preview the worksheet, and then submit your work to your instructor as directed. (*Hint:* Change the Zoom factor to 100% by clicking the Zoom out button twice.)

**FIGURE B-28**

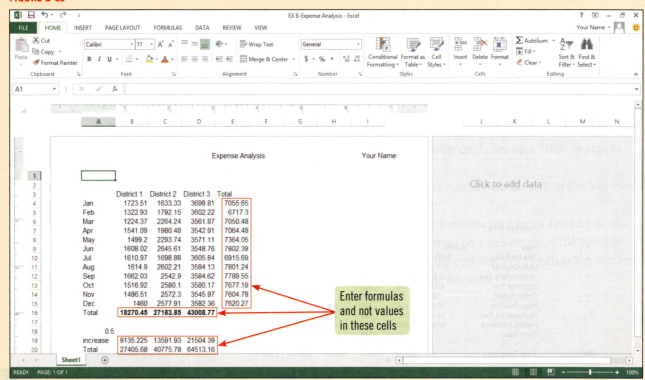

# Formatting a Worksheet

**CASE** ▶ The corporate marketing managers at QST have requested data from all QST locations for advertising expenses incurred during the first quarter of this year. Grace Wong has created a worksheet listing this information. She asks you to format the worksheet to make it easier to read and to call attention to important data.

## Unit Objectives

After completing this unit, you will be able to:

- Format values
- Change font and font size
- Change font styles and alignment
- Adjust the column width
- Insert and delete rows and columns
- Apply colors, patterns, and borders
- Apply conditional formatting
- Rename and move a worksheet
- Check spelling

## Files You Will Need

EX C-1.xlsx
EX C-2.xlsx
EX C-3.xlsx
EX C-4.xlsx
EX C-5.xlsx

©Katerina Havelkova/Shutterstock

# Format Values

Learning
Outcomes
• Format a number
• Format a date
• Increase/decrease
  decimals

The **format** of a cell determines how the labels and values look—for example, whether the contents appear boldfaced, italicized, or with dollar signs and commas. Formatting changes only the appearance of a value or label; it does not alter the actual data in any way. To format a cell or range, first you select it, then you apply the formatting using the Ribbon, Mini toolbar, or a keyboard shortcut. You can apply formatting before or after you enter data in a cell or range. **CASE** ▶ *Grace has provided you with a worksheet that details advertising expenses, and you're ready to improve its appearance and readability. You start by formatting some of the values so they are displayed as currency, percentages, and dates.*

## STEPS

1. **Start Excel, open the file EX C-1.xlsx from the location where you store your Data Files, then save it as EX C-QST Advertising Expenses**

   This worksheet is difficult to interpret because all the information is crowded and looks the same. In some columns, the contents appear cut off because there is too much data to fit given the current column width. You decide not to widen the columns yet, because the other changes you plan to make might affect column width and row height. The first thing you want to do is format the data showing the cost of each ad.

**QUICK TIP**

You can use a different type of currency, such as Euros or British pounds, by clicking the Accounting Number Format list arrow, then clicking a different currency type.

2. **Select the range D4:D32, then click the Accounting Number Format button $ in the Number group on the HOME tab**

   The default Accounting **number format** adds dollar signs and two decimal places to the data, as shown in **FIGURE C-1**. Formatting this data in Accounting format makes it clear that its values are monetary values. Excel automatically resizes the column to display the new formatting. The Accounting and Currency number formats are both used for monetary values, but the Accounting format aligns currency symbols and decimal points of numbers in a column.

**QUICK TIP**

Select any range of contiguous cells by clicking the upper-left cell of the range, pressing and holding [Shift], then clicking the lower-right cell of the range. Add a column to the selected range by continuing to hold down [Shift] and pressing ➡; add a row by pressing ⬇.

3. **Select the range F4:H32, then click the Comma Style button ▾ in the Number group**

   The values in columns F, G, and H display the Comma Style format, which does not include a dollar sign but can be useful for some types of accounting data.

4. **Select the range J4:J32, click the Number Format list arrow, click Percentage, then click the Increase Decimal button ⬆ in the Number group**

   The data in the % of Total column is now formatted with a percent sign (%) and three decimal places. The Number Format list arrow lets you choose from popular number formats and shows an example of what the selected cell or cells would look like in each format (when multiple cells are selected, the example is based on the first cell in the range). Each time you click the Increase Decimal button, you add one decimal place; clicking the button twice would add two decimal places.

5. **Click the Decrease Decimal button ⬇ in the Number group twice**

   Two decimal places are removed from the percentage values in column J.

6. **Select the range B4:B31, then click the dialog box launcher ⌐ in the Number group**

   The Format Cells dialog box opens with the Date category already selected on the Number tab.

7. **Select the first 14-Mar-12 format in the Type list box as shown in FIGURE C-2, then click OK**

   The dates in column B appear in the 14-Mar-12 format. The second 14-Mar-12 format in the list (visible if you scroll down the list) displays all days in two digits (it adds a leading zero if the day is only a single-digit number), while the one you chose displays single-digit days without a leading zero.

**QUICK TIP**

Make sure you examine formatted data to confirm that you have applied the appropriate formatting; for example, dates should not have a currency format, and monetary values should not have a date format.

8. **Select the range C4:C31, right-click the range, click Format Cells on the shortcut menu, click 14-Mar in the Type list box in the Format Cells dialog box, then click OK**

   Compare your worksheet to **FIGURE C-3**.

9. **Press [Ctrl][Home], then save your work**

Formatting a Worksheet

**FIGURE C-1:** Accounting number format applied to range

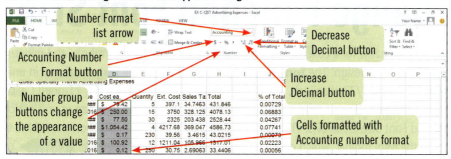

**FIGURE C-2:** Format Cells dialog box

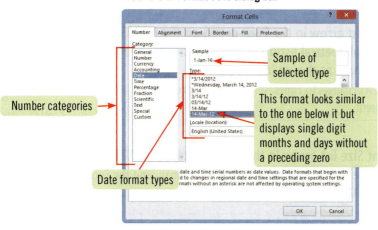

**FIGURE C-3:** Worksheet with formatted values

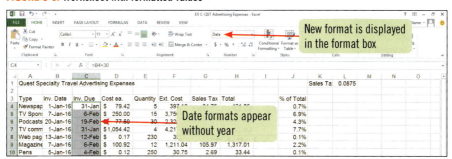

## Formatting as a table

Excel includes 60 predefined **table styles** to make it easy to format selected worksheet cells as a table. You can apply table styles to any range of cells that you want to format quickly, or even to an entire worksheet, but they're especially useful for those ranges with labels in the left column and top row, and totals in the bottom row or right column. To apply a table style, select the data to be formatted or click anywhere within the intended range (Excel can automatically detect a range of cells filled with data), click the Format as Table button in the Styles group on the HOME tab, then click a style in the gallery, as shown in **FIGURE C-4**. Table styles are organized in three categories: Light, Medium, and Dark. Once you click a style, Excel asks you to confirm the range selection, then applies the style. Once you have formatted a range as a table, you can use Live Preview to preview the table in other styles by pointing to any style in the Table Styles gallery.

**FIGURE C-4:** Table Styles gallery

# Change Font Styles and Alignment

**Font styles** are formats such as bold, italic, and underlining that you can apply to affect the way text and numbers look in a worksheet. You can also change the **alignment** of labels and values in cells to position them in relation to the cells' edges—such as left-aligned, right-aligned, or centered. You can apply font styles and alignment options using the HOME tab, the Format Cells dialog box, or the Mini toolbar. See **TABLE C-2** for a description of common font style and alignment buttons that are available on the HOME tab and the Mini toolbar. Once you have formatted a cell the way you want it, you can "paint" or copy the cell's formats into other cells by using the Format Painter button in the Clipboard group on the HOME tab. This is similar to using copy and paste, but instead of copying cell contents, it copies only the cell's formatting. **CASE** *You want to further enhance the worksheet's appearance by adding bold and underline formatting and centering some of the labels.*

## STEPS

**QUICK TIP**
You can use the following keyboard shortcuts to format a selected cell or range: [Ctrl][B] to bold, [Ctrl][I] to italicize, and [Ctrl][U] to underline.

1. **Press [Ctrl][Home], then click the Bold button** B **in the Font group on the HOME tab**
   The title in cell A1 appears in bold.

2. **Click cell A3, then click the Underline button** U **in the Font group**
   The column label is now underlined, though this may be difficult to see with the cell selected.

3. **Click the Italic button** I **in the Font group, then click** B
   The heading now appears in boldface, underlined, italic type. Notice that the Bold, Italic, and Underline buttons in the Font group are all selected.

**QUICK TIP**
Overuse of any font style and random formatting can make a workbook difficult to read. Be consistent and add the same formatting to similar items throughout a worksheet or in related worksheets.

4. **Click the Italic button** I **to deselect it**
   The italic font style is removed from cell A3, but the bold and underline font styles remain.

5. **Click the Format Painter button** 🖌 **in the Clipboard group, then select the range B3:J3**
   The formatting in cell A3 is copied to the rest of the column labels. To paint the formats on more than one selection, double-click the Format Painter button to keep it activated until you turn it off. You can turn off the Format Painter by pressing [Esc] or by clicking 🖌. You decide the title would look better if it were centered over the data columns.

6. **Select the range A1:H1, then click the Merge & Center button** 📑 **in the Alignment group**
   The Merge & Center button creates one cell out of the eight cells across the row, then centers the text in that newly created, merged cell. The title "Quest Specialty Travel Advertising Expenses" is centered across the eight columns you selected. To split a merged cell into its original components, select the merged cell, then click the Merge & Center button to deselect it. The merged and centered text might look awkward now, but you'll be changing the column widths shortly. Occasionally, you may find that you want cell contents to wrap within a cell. You can do this by selecting the cells containing the text you want to wrap, then clicking the Wrap Text button 📑 in the Alignment group on the HOME tab on the Ribbon.

**QUICK TIP**
To clear all formatting from a selected range, click the Clear button 🧹 in the Editing group on the HOME tab, then click Clear Formats.

7. **Select the range A3:J3, right-click, then click the Center button** ≡ **on the Mini toolbar**
   Compare your screen to **FIGURE C-8**. Although they may be difficult to read, notice that all the headings are centered within their cells.

8. **Save your work**

**FIGURE C-8:** Worksheet with font styles and alignment applied

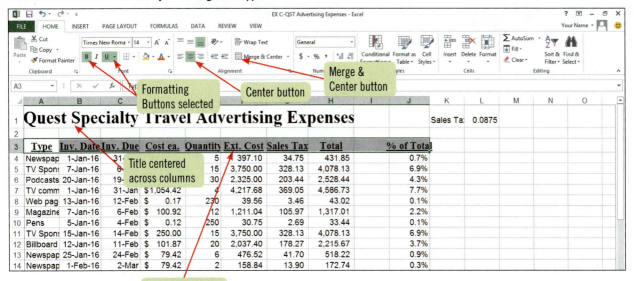

**TABLE C-2:** Common font style and alignment buttons

| button | description |
|---|---|
| **B** | Bolds text |
| *I* | Italicizes text |
| U | Underlines text |
| | Centers text across columns, and combines two or more selected, adjacent cells into one cell |
| | Aligns text at the left edge of the cell |
| | Centers text horizontally within the cell |
| | Aligns text at the right edge of the cell |
| | Wraps long text into multiple lines |

## Rotating and indenting cell entries

In addition to applying fonts and font styles, you can rotate or indent data within a cell to further change its appearance. You can rotate text within a cell by altering its alignment. To change alignment, select the cells you want to modify, then click the dialog box launcher in the Alignment group to open the Alignment tab of the Format Cells dialog box. Click a position in the Orientation box or type a number in the Degrees text box to rotate text from its default horizontal orientation, then click OK. You can indent cell contents using the Increase Indent button in the Alignment group, which moves cell contents to the right one space, or the Decrease Indent button, which moves cell contents to the left one space.

# Adjust the Column Width

**Learning Outcomes**
• Change a column width by dragging
• Resize a column with AutoFit
• Change the width of multiple columns

As you format a worksheet, you might need to adjust the width of one or more columns to accommodate changes in the amount of text, the font size, or font style. The default column width is 8.43 characters, a little less than 1". With Excel, you can adjust the width of one or more columns by using the mouse, the Format button in the Cells group on the HOME tab, or the shortcut menu. Using the mouse, you can drag or double-click the right edge of a column heading. The Format button and shortcut menu include commands for making more precise width adjustments. **TABLE C-3** describes common column formatting commands. **CASE** ▶ *You have noticed that some of the labels in columns A through J don't fit in the cells. You want to adjust the widths of the columns so that the labels appear in their entirety.*

## STEPS

1. **Position the mouse pointer on the line between the column A and column B headings until it changes to ↔**

   See **FIGURE C-9**. The **column heading** is the box at the top of each column containing a letter. Before you can adjust column width using the mouse, you need to position the pointer on the right edge of the column heading for the column you want to adjust. The cell entry "TV commercials" is the widest in the column.

2. **Click and drag the ↔ to the right until the column displays the "TV commercials" cell entries fully (approximately 15.29 characters, 1.23", or 112 pixels)**

   As you change the column width, a ScreenTip is displayed listing the column width. In Normal view, the ScreenTip lists the width in characters and pixels; in Page Layout view, the ScreenTip lists the width in inches and pixels.

3. **Position the pointer on the line between columns B and C until it changes to ↔, then double-click**

   Double-clicking the right edge of a column heading activates the **AutoFit** feature, which automatically resizes the column to accommodate the widest entry in the column. Column B automatically widens to fit the widest entry, which is the column label "Inv. Date".

4. **Use AutoFit to resize columns C, D, and J**

5. **Select the range E5:H5**

   You can change the width of multiple columns at once, by first selecting either the column headings or at least one cell in each column.

6. **Click the Format button in the Cells group, then click Column Width**

   The Column Width dialog box opens. Column width measurement is based on the number of characters that will fit in the column when formatted in the Normal font and font size (in this case, 11 pt Calibri).

7. **Drag the dialog box by its title bar if its placement obscures your view of the worksheet, type 11 in the Column width text box, then click OK**

   The widths of columns E, F, G, and H change to reflect the new setting. See **FIGURE C-10**.

8. **Save your work**

**FIGURE C-9:** Preparing to change the column width

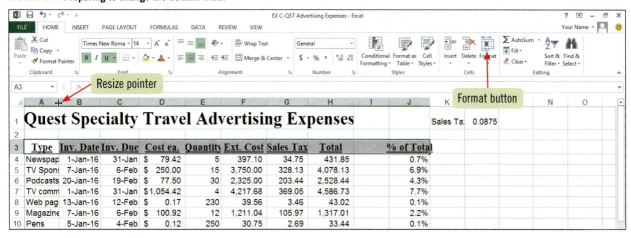

**FIGURE C-10:** Worksheet with column widths adjusted

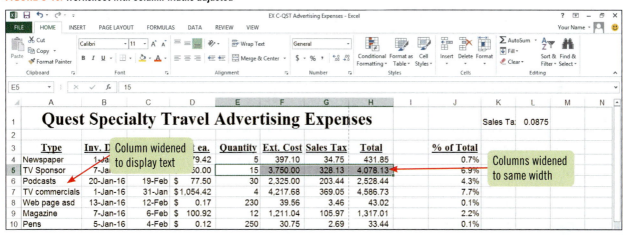

**TABLE C-3:** Common column formatting commands

| command | description | available using |
|---|---|---|
| Column Width | Sets the width to a specific number of characters | Format button; shortcut menu |
| AutoFit Column Width | Fits to the widest entry in a column | Format button; mouse |
| Hide & Unhide | Hides or displays hidden column(s) | Format button; shortcut menu |
| Default Width | Resets column to worksheet's default column width | Format button |

### Changing row height

Changing row height is as easy as changing column width. Row height is calculated in points, the same units of measure used for fonts. The row height must exceed the size of the font you are using. Normally, you don't need to adjust row heights manually, because row heights adjust automatically to accommodate font size changes. If you format something in a row to be a larger point size, Excel adjusts the row to fit the largest point size in the row. However, you have just as many options for changing row height as you do column width. Using the mouse, you can place the ✛ pointer on the line dividing a row heading from the heading below, and then drag to the desired height; double-clicking the line AutoFits the row height where necessary. You can also select one or more rows, then use the Row Height command on the shortcut menu, or click the Format button on the HOME tab and click the Row Height or AutoFit Row Height command.

**Learning Outcomes**
• Use the Insert dialog box
• Use column and row heading buttons to insert and delete

# Insert and Delete Rows and Columns

As you modify a worksheet, you might find it necessary to insert or delete rows and columns to keep your worksheet current. For example, you might need to insert rows to accommodate new inventory products or remove a column of yearly totals that are no longer necessary. When you insert a new row, the row is inserted above the cell pointer and the contents of the worksheet shift down from the newly inserted row. When you insert a new column, the column is inserted to the left of the cell pointer and the contents of the worksheet shift to the right of the new column. To insert multiple rows, select the same number of row headings as you want to insert before using the Insert command. **CASE** *You want to improve the overall appearance of the worksheet by inserting a row between the last row of data and the totals. Also, you have learned that row 27 and column J need to be deleted from the worksheet.*

## STEPS

1. **Right-click cell A32, then click Insert on the shortcut menu**

   The Insert dialog box opens. See **FIGURE C-11**. You can choose to insert a column or a row; insert a single cell and shift the cells in the active column to the right; or insert a single cell and shift the cells in the active row down. An additional row between the last row of data and the totals will visually separate the totals.

2. **Click the Entire row option button, then click OK**

   A blank row appears between the Billboard data and the totals, and the formula result in cell E33 has not changed. The Insert Options button appears beside cell A33. Pointing to the button displays a list arrow, which you can click and then choose from the following options: Format Same As Above (the default setting, already selected), Format Same As Below, or Clear Formatting.

3. **Click the row 27 heading**

   All of row 27 is selected, as shown in **FIGURE C-12**.

4. **Click the Delete button in the Cells group; *do not click the list arrow***

   Excel deletes row 27, and all rows below it shift up one row. You must use the Delete button or the Delete command on the shortcut menu to delete a row or column; pressing [Delete] on the keyboard removes only the *contents* of a selected row or column.

5. **Click the column J heading**

   The percentage information is calculated elsewhere and is no longer necessary in this worksheet.

6. **Click the Delete button in the Cells group**

   Excel deletes column J. The remaining columns to the right shift left one column.

7. **Use AutoFit to resize columns F and H, then save your work**

**QUICK TIP**
To insert a single row or column, right-click the row heading immediately below where you want the new row, or right-click the column heading to the right of where you want the new column, then click Insert on the shortcut menu.

**QUICK TIP**
If you inadvertently click the Delete list arrow instead of the button itself, click Delete Sheet Rows in the menu that opens.

**QUICK TIP**
After inserting or deleting rows or columns in a worksheet, be sure to proof formulas that contain relative cell references.

Formatting a Worksheet

**FIGURE C-11:** Insert dialog box

**FIGURE C-11:** Insert dialog box

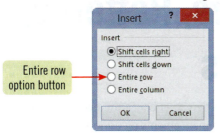

Entire row
option button

**FIGURE C-12:** Worksheet with row 27 selected

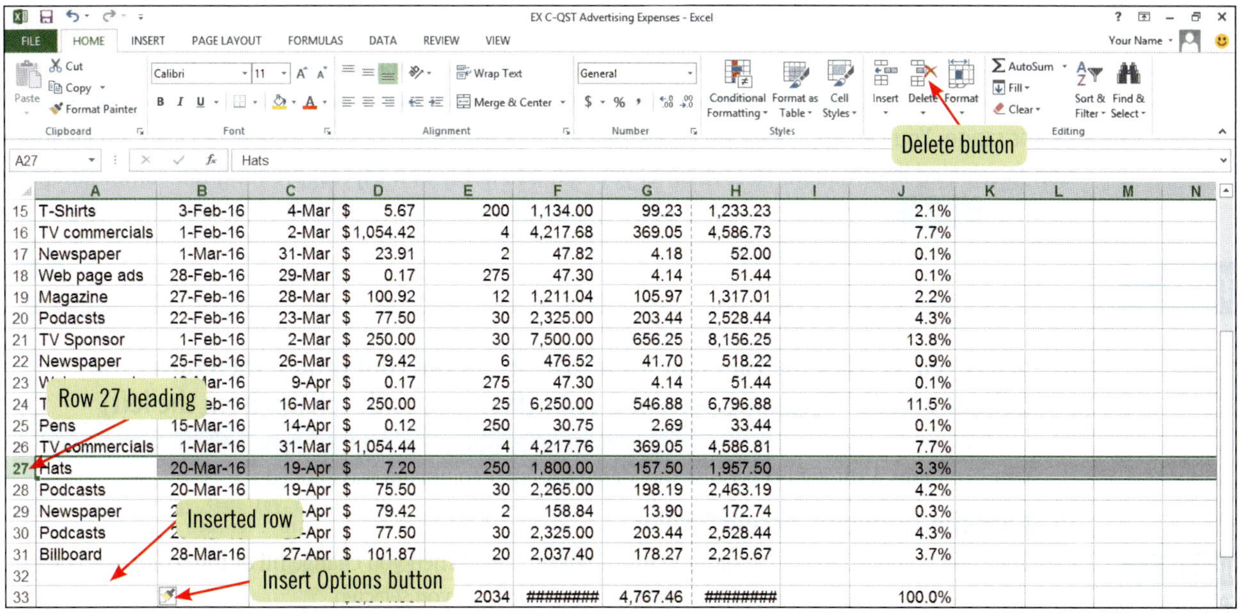

Row 27 heading

Inserted row

Insert Options button

Delete button

## Hiding and unhiding columns and rows

When you don't want data in a column or row to be visible, but you don't want to delete it, you can hide the column or row. To hide a selected column, click the Format button in the Cells group on the HOME tab, point to Hide & Unhide, then click Hide Columns. A hidden column is indicated by a dark green vertical line in its original position. This green line disappears when you click elsewhere in the worksheet. You can display a hidden column by selecting the columns on either side of the hidden column, clicking the Format button in the Cells group, pointing to Hide & Unhide, and then clicking Unhide Columns. (To hide or unhide one or more rows, substitute Hide Rows and Unhide Rows for the Hide Columns and Unhide Columns commands.)

## Adding and editing comments

Much of your work in Excel may be in collaboration with team-mates with whom you share worksheets. You can share ideas with other worksheet users by adding comments within selected cells. To include a comment in a worksheet, click the cell where you want to place the comment, click the REVIEW tab on the Ribbon, then click the New Comment button in the Comments group. You can type your comments in the resizable text box that opens containing the computer user's name. A small, red triangle appears in the upper-right corner of a cell containing a comment. If comments are not already displayed in a workbook, other users can point to the triangle to display the comment. To see all worksheet comments, as shown in **FIGURE C-13**, click the Show All Comments button in the Comments group. To edit a comment, click the cell containing the comment, then click the Edit Comment button in the Comments group. To delete a comment, click the cell containing the comment, then click the Delete button in the Comments group.

**FIGURE C-13:** Comments displayed in a worksheet

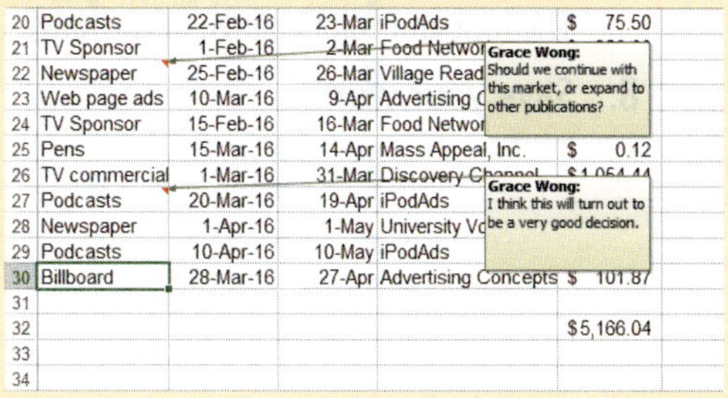

Excel 2013

# Apply Conditional Formatting

So far, you've used formatting to change the appearance of different types of data, but you can also use formatting to highlight important aspects of the data itself. For example, you can apply formatting that changes the font color to red for any cells where ad costs exceed $100 and to green where ad costs are below $50. This is called **conditional formatting** because Excel automatically applies different formats to data if the data meets conditions you specify. The formatting is updated if you change data in the worksheet. You can also copy conditional formats the same way you copy other formats. **CASE** ▶ *Grace is concerned about advertising costs exceeding the yearly budget. You decide to use conditional formatting to highlight certain trends and patterns in the data so that it's easy to spot the most expensive advertising.*

## STEPS

1. **Select the range H4:H30, click the Conditional Formatting button in the Styles group on the HOME tab, point to Data Bars, then point to the Light Blue Data Bar (second row, second from left)**

   Data bars are colored horizontal bars that visually illustrate differences between values in a range of cells. Live Preview shows how this formatting will appear in the worksheet, as shown in **FIGURE C-17**.

2. **Point to the Green Data Bar (first row, second from left), then click it**

3. **Select the range F4:F30, click the Conditional Formatting button in the Styles group, then point to Highlight Cells Rules**

   The Highlight Cells Rules submenu displays choices for creating different formatting conditions. For example, you can create a rule for values that are greater than or less than a certain amount, or between two amounts.

4. **Click Between on the submenu**

   The Between dialog box opens, displaying input boxes you can use to define the condition and a default format (Light Red Fill with Dark Red Text) selected for cells that meet that condition. Depending on the condition you select in the Highlight Cells Rules submenu (such as "Greater Than" or "Less Than"), this dialog box displays different input boxes. You define the condition using the input boxes and then assign the formatting you want to use for cells that meet that condition. Values used in input boxes for a condition can be constants, formulas, cell references, or dates.

5. **Type 2000 in the first text box, type 4000 in the second text box, click the with list arrow, click Light Red Fill, compare your settings to FIGURE C-18, then click OK**

   All cells with values between 2000 and 4000 in column F appear with a light red fill.

6. **Click cell F7, type 3975.55, then press [Enter]**

   When the value in cell F7 changes, the formatting also changes because the new value meets the condition you set. Compare your results to **FIGURE C-19**.

7. **Press [Ctrl][Home] to select cell A1, then save your work**

**FIGURE C-17:** Previewing data bars in a range

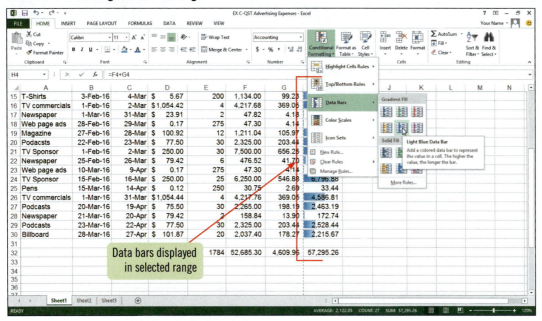

**FIGURE C-18:** Between dialog box

**FIGURE C-19:** Worksheet with conditional formatting

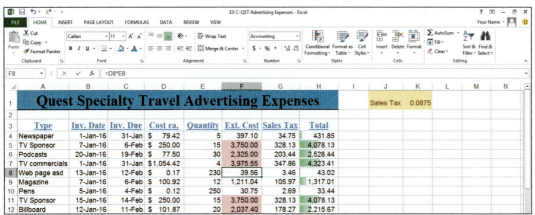

## Managing conditional formatting rules

If you create a conditional formatting rule and then want to change the condition to reflect a different value or format, you don't need to create a new rule; instead, you can modify the rule using the Rules Manager. Select the cell(s) containing conditional formatting, click the Conditional Formatting button in the Styles group, then click Manage Rules. The Conditional Formatting Rules Manager dialog box opens. Select the rule you want to edit, click Edit Rule, and then modify the settings in the Edit the Rule Description area in the Edit Formatting Rule dialog box. To change

the formatting for a rule, click the Format button in the Edit the Rule Description area, select the formatting styles you want the text to have, then click OK three times to close the Format Cells dialog box, the Edit Formatting Rule dialog box, and then the Conditional Formatting Rules Manager dialog box. The rule is modified, and the new conditional formatting is applied to the selected cells. To delete a rule, select the rule in the Conditional Formatting Rules Manager dialog box, then click the Delete Rule button.

# Rename and Move a Worksheet

**Learning Outcomes**
• Rename a sheet
• Apply color to a sheet tab
• Reorder sheets in a workbook

By default, an Excel workbook initially contains one worksheet named Sheet1, although you can add sheets at any time. Each sheet name appears on a sheet tab at the bottom of the worksheet. When you open a new workbook, the first worksheet, Sheet1, is the active sheet. To move from sheet to sheet, you can click any sheet tab at the bottom of the worksheet window. The sheet tab scrolling buttons, located to the left of the sheet tabs, are useful when a workbook contains too many sheet tabs to display at once. To make it easier to identify the sheets in a workbook, you can rename each sheet and add color to the tabs. You can also organize them in a logical way. For instance, to better track performance goals, you could name each workbook sheet for an individual salesperson, and you could move the sheets so they appear in alphabetical order. **CASE** *In the current worksheet, Sheet1 contains information about actual advertising expenses. Sheet2 contains an advertising budget, and Sheet3 contains no data. You want to rename the two sheets in the workbook to reflect their contents, add color to a sheet tab to easily distinguish one from the other, and change their order.*

## STEPS

1. **Click the Sheet2 tab**

   Sheet2 becomes active, appearing in front of the Sheet1 tab; this is the worksheet that contains the budgeted advertising expenses. See **FIGURE C-20**.

**QUICK TIP**
You can also rename a sheet by right-clicking the tab, clicking Rename on the shortcut menu, typing the new name, then pressing [Enter].

2. **Click the Sheet1 tab**

   Sheet1, which contains the actual advertising expenses, becomes active again.

3. **Double-click the Sheet2 tab, type Budget, then press [Enter]**

   The new name for Sheet2 automatically replaces the default name on the tab. Worksheet names can have up to 31 characters, including spaces and punctuation.

**QUICK TIP**
To delete a sheet, click its tab, click the Delete list arrow in the Cells group, then click Delete Sheet. To insert a worksheet, click the New sheet button ⊕ to the right of the sheet tabs.

4. **Right-click the Budget tab, point to Tab Color on the shortcut menu, then click the Bright Green, Accent 4, Lighter 40% color (fourth row, third column from the right) as shown in FIGURE C-21**

5. **Double-click the Sheet1 tab, type Actual, then press [Enter]**

   Notice that the color of the Budget tab changes depending on whether it is the active tab; when the Actual tab is active, the color of the Budget tab changes to the green tab color you selected. You decide to rearrange the order of the sheets, so that the Budget tab is to the left of the Actual tab.

**QUICK TIP**
If you have more sheet tabs than are visible, you can move between sheets by using the tab scrolling buttons to the left of the sheet tabs: the Previous Worksheet button ◀ and the Next Worksheet button ▶.

6. **Click the Budget tab, hold down the mouse button, drag it to the left of the Actual tab, as shown in FIGURE C-22, then release the mouse button**

   As you drag, the pointer changes to ⬚, the sheet relocation pointer, and a small, black triangle just above the tabs shows the position the moved sheet will be in when you release the mouse button. The first sheet in the workbook is now the Budget sheet. See **FIGURE C-23**. You can move multiple sheets by pressing and holding [Shift] while clicking the sheets you want to move, then dragging the sheets to their new location.

7. **Click the Actual sheet tab, click the Page Layout button 🔲 on the status bar to open Page Layout view, enter your name in the left header text box, then click anywhere in the worksheet to deselect the header**

8. **Click the PAGE LAYOUT tab on the Ribbon, click the Orientation button in the Page Setup group, then click Landscape**

9. **Right-click the Sheet3 tab, click Delete on the shortcut menu, press [Ctrl][Home], then save your work**

**FIGURE C-20:** Sheet tabs in workbook

Sheet1 tab    Sheet2 tab

**FIGURE C-21:** Tab Color palette

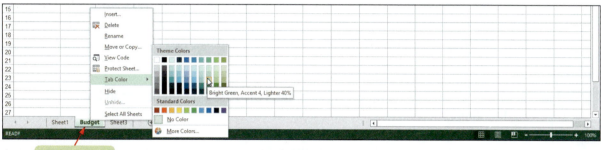

Sheet2 renamed

**FIGURE C-22:** Moving the Budget sheet

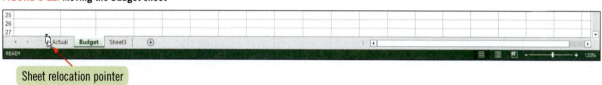

Sheet relocation pointer

**FIGURE C-23:** Reordered sheets

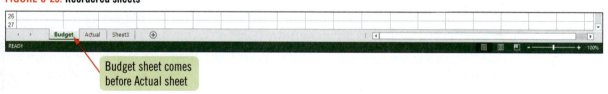

Budget sheet comes
before Actual sheet

## Copying, Adding, and Deleting worksheets

There are times when you may want to copy a worksheet. For example, a workbook might contain a sheet with Quarter 1 expenses, and you want to use that sheet as the basis for a sheet containing Quarter 2 expenses. To copy a sheet within the same workbook, press and hold [Ctrl], drag the sheet tab to the desired tab location, release the mouse button, then release [Ctrl]. A duplicate sheet appears with the same name as the copied sheet followed by "(2)" indicating it is a copy. You can then rename the sheet to a more meaningful name. To copy a sheet to a different workbook, both the source and destination workbooks must be open. Select the sheet to copy or move, right-click the sheet tab, then click Move or Copy in the shortcut menu. Complete the information in the Move or Copy dialog box. Be sure to click the Create a copy check box if you are copying rather than moving the worksheet. Carefully check your calculation results whenever you move or copy a worksheet. You can add multiple worksheets to a workbook by clicking the HOME tab on the Ribbon, pressing and holding [Shift], then clicking the number of existing worksheet tabs that correspond with the number of sheets you want to add, clicking the Insert list arrow in the Cells group on the HOME tab, then clicking Insert Sheet. You can delete multiple worksheets from a workbook by clicking the HOME tab on the Ribbon, pressing and holding [Shift], clicking the sheet tabs of the worksheets you want to delete, clicking the Delete list arrow in the Cells group on the HOME tab, then clicking Delete Sheet.

# Check Spelling

Excel includes a spell checker to help you ensure that the words in your worksheet are spelled correctly. The spell checker scans your worksheet, displays words it doesn't find in its built-in dictionary, and suggests replacements when they are available. To check all of the sheets in a multiple-sheet workbook, you need to display each sheet individually and run the spell checker for each one. Because the built-in dictionary cannot possibly include all the words that anyone needs, you can add words to the dictionary, such as your company name, an acronym, or an unusual technical term. Once you add a word or term, the spell checker no longer considers that word misspelled. Any words you've added to the dictionary using Word, Access, or PowerPoint are also available in Excel. **CASE** ▶ *Before you distribute this workbook to Grace and the marketing managers, you check its spelling.*

## STEPS

1. **Click the REVIEW tab on the Ribbon, then click the Spelling button in the Proofing group**

   The Spelling: English (U.S.) dialog box opens, as shown in **FIGURE C-24**, with "asd" selected as the first misspelled word in the worksheet, and with "ads" selected in the Suggestions list as a possible replacement. For any word, you have the option to Ignore this case of the flagged word, Ignore All cases of the flagged word, Change the word to the selected suggestion, Change All instances of the flagged word to the selected suggestion, or add the flagged word to the dictionary using Add to Dictionary.

2. **Click Change**

   Next, the spell checker finds the word "Podacsts" and suggests "Podcasts" as an alternative.

3. **Verify that the word Podcasts is selected in the Suggestions list, then click Change**

   When no more incorrect words are found, Excel displays a message indicating that the spell check is complete.

4. **Click OK**

5. **Click the HOME tab, click Find & Select in the Editing group, then click Replace**

   The Find and Replace dialog box opens. You can use this dialog box to replace a word or phrase. It might be a misspelling of a proper name that the spell checker didn't recognize as misspelled, or it could simply be a term that you want to change throughout the worksheet. Grace has just told you that each instance of "Billboard" in the worksheet should be changed to "Sign."

6. **Type Billboard in the Find what text box, press [Tab], then type Sign in the Replace with text box**

   Compare your dialog box to **FIGURE C-25**.

7. **Click Replace All, click OK to close the Microsoft Excel dialog box, then click Close to close the Find and Replace dialog box**

   Excel has made two replacements.

8. **Click the FILE tab, click Print on the navigation bar, click the No Scaling setting in the Settings section on the Print tab, then click Fit Sheet on One Page**

9. **Click the Return button to return to your worksheet, save your work, submit it to your instructor as directed, close the workbook, then exit Excel**

   The completed worksheet is shown in **FIGURE C-26**.

---

### Emailing a workbook

You can send an entire workbook from within Excel using your installed email program, such as Microsoft Outlook. To send a workbook as an email message attachment, open the workbook, click the FILE tab, then click Share on the navigation bar. With the Email option selected in the Share section in Backstage view, click Send as Attachment in the right pane. An email message opens in your default email program with the workbook automatically attached; the filename appears in the Attached field. Complete the To and optional Cc fields, include a message if you wish, then click Send.

**FIGURE C-24:** Spelling: English (U.S.) dialog box

Misspelled word → 

Click to ignore all occurrences of misspelled word

Click to add word to dictionary

Suggested replacements for misspelled word

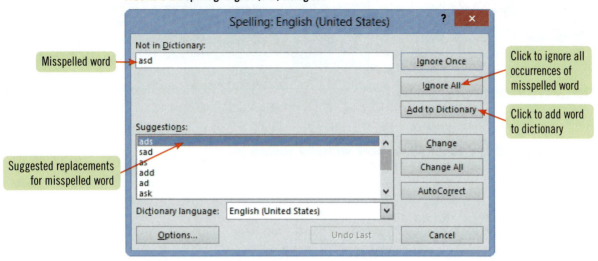

**FIGURE C-25:** Find and Replace dialog box

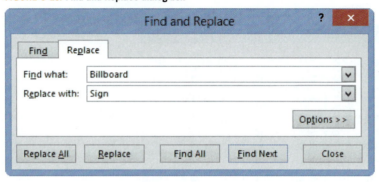

**FIGURE C-26:** Completed worksheet

Your Name

## Quest Specialty Travel Advertising Expenses

Sales Tax

| Type | Inv. Date | Inv. Due | Cost ea. | Quantity | Ext. Cost | Sales Tax | Total |
|------|-----------|----------|----------|----------|-----------|-----------|-------|
| Newspaper | 1-Jan-16 | 31-Jan | $ 79.42 | 5 | 397.10 | 34.75 | 431.85 |
| TV Sponsor | 7-Jan-16 | 6-Feb | $ 250.00 | 15 | 3,750.00 | 328.13 | 4,078.13 |
| Podcasts | 20-Jan-16 | 19-Feb | $ 77.50 | 30 | 2,325.00 | 203.44 | 2,528.44 |
| TV commercials | 1-Jan-16 | 31-Jan | $ 1,054.42 | 4 | 3,975.55 | 347.86 | 4,323.41 |
| Web page ads | 13-Jan-16 | 12-Feb | $ 0.17 | 230 | 39.56 | 3.46 | 43.02 |
| Magazine | 7-Jan-16 | 6-Feb | $ 100.92 | 12 | 1,211.04 | 105.97 | 1,317.01 |
| Pens | 5-Jan-16 | 4-Feb | $ 0.12 | 250 | 30.75 | 2.69 | 33.44 |
| TV Sponsor | 15-Jan-16 | 14-Feb | $ 250.00 | 15 | 3,750.00 | 328.13 | 4,078.13 |
| Sign | 12-Jan-16 | 11-Feb | $ 101.87 | 20 | 2,037.40 | 178.27 | 2,215.67 |
| Newspaper | 25-Jan-16 | 24-Feb | $ 79.42 | 6 | 476.52 | 41.70 | 518.22 |
| Newspaper | 1-Feb-16 | 2-Mar | $ 79.42 | 2 | 158.84 | 13.90 | 172.74 |
| T-Shirts | 3-Feb-16 | 4-Mar | $ 5.67 | 200 | 1,134.00 | 99.23 | 1,233.23 |
| TV commercials | 1-Feb-16 | 2-Mar | $ 1,054.42 | 4 | 4,217.68 | 369.05 | 4,586.73 |
| Newspaper | 1-Mar-16 | 31-Mar | $ 23.91 | 2 | 47.82 | 4.18 | 52.00 |
| Web page ads | 28-Feb-16 | 29-Mar | $ 0.17 | 275 | 47.30 | 4.14 | 51.44 |
| Magazine | 27-Feb-16 | 28-Mar | $ 100.92 | 12 | 1,211.04 | 105.97 | 1,317.01 |
| Podcasts | 22-Feb-16 | 23-Mar | $ 77.50 | 30 | 2,325.00 | 203.44 | 2,528.44 |
| TV Sponsor | 1-Feb-16 | 2-Mar | $ 250.00 | 30 | 7,500.00 | 656.25 | 8,156.25 |
| Newspaper | 25-Feb-16 | 26-Mar | $ 79.42 | 6 | 476.52 | 41.70 | 518.22 |
| Web page ads | 10-Mar-16 | 9-Apr | $ 0.17 | 275 | 47.30 | 4.14 | 51.44 |
| TV Sponsor | 15-Feb-16 | 16-Mar | $ 250.00 | 25 | 6,250.00 | 546.88 | 6,796.88 |
| Pens | 15-Mar-16 | 14-Apr | $ 0.12 | 250 | 30.75 | 2.69 | 33.44 |
| TV commercials | 1-Mar-16 | 31-Mar | $ 1,054.44 | 4 | 4,217.76 | 369.05 | 4,586.81 |
| Podcasts | 20-Mar-16 | 19-Apr | $ 75.50 | 30 | 2,265.00 | 198.19 | 2,463.19 |
| Newspaper | 21-Mar-16 | 20-Apr | $ 79.42 | 2 | 158.84 | 13.90 | 172.74 |
| Podcasts | 23-Mar-16 | 22-Apr | $ 77.50 | 30 | 2,325.00 | 203.44 | 2,528.44 |
| Sign | 28-Mar-16 | 27-Apr | $ 101.87 | 20 | 2,037.40 | 178.27 | 2,215.67 |
| | | | $ 5,304.30 | 1784 | 52,443.17 | 4,588.78 | 57,031.95 |

# Practice

## Concepts Review

**Label each element of the Excel worksheet window shown in FIGURE C-27.**

FIGURE C-27

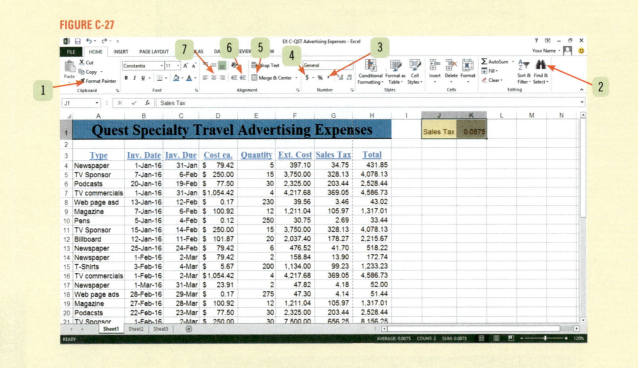

**Match each command or button with the statement that best describes it.**

8. **Conditional formatting**
9. $ \boxed{\$} $
10. **Spelling button**
11. **[Ctrl][Home]**
12. ▦
13. ◇ ▾

a. Checks for apparent misspellings in a worksheet
b. Adds dollar signs and two decimal places to selected data
c. Centers cell contents over multiple cells
d. Changes formatting of a cell that meets a certain rule
e. Moves cell pointer to cell A1
f. Displays background color options for a cell

**Select the best answer from the list of choices.**

14. Which button increases the number of decimal places in selected cells?
    - **a.** [button: ←.0 .00]
    - **b.** [button: .00 →.0]
    - **c.** [button]
    - **d.** [button]

15. What feature is used to delete a conditional formatting rule?
    - **a.** Rules Reminder
    - **b.** Conditional Formatting Rules Manager
    - **c.** Condition Manager
    - **d.** Format Manager

16. Which button removes the italic font style from selected cells?
    - **a.** [button: *I*]
    - **b.** [button: B]
    - **c.** [button: *I* highlighted]
    - **d.** [button: U]

17. Which button copies multiple formats from selected cells to other cells?
    - **a.** [button]
    - **b.** [button]
    - **c.** [button: A]
    - **d.** [button]

18. What is the name of the feature used to resize a column to accommodate its widest entry?
    - **a.** AutoFormat
    - **b.** AutoFit
    - **c.** AutoResize
    - **d.** AutoRefit

19. Which of the following is an example of Accounting number format?
    - **a.** 5555
    - **b.** $5,555.55
    - **c.** 55.55%
    - **d.** 5,555.55

# Skills Review

1. **Format values.**
   a. Start Excel, open the file EX C-2.xlsx from the location where you store your Data Files, then save it as **EX C-Life Insurance Premiums**.
   b. Use the Sum function to enter a formula in cell B10 that totals the number of employees.
   c. Create a formula in cell C5 that calculates the monthly insurance premium for the accounting department. (*Hint*: Make sure you use the correct type of cell reference in the formula. To calculate the department's monthly premium, multiply the number of employees by the monthly premium in cell B14.)
   d. Copy the formula in cell C5 to the range C6:C10.
   e. Format the range C5:C10 using Accounting number format.
   f. Change the format of the range C6:C9 to the Comma Style.
   g. Reduce the number of decimals in cell B14 to 0 using a button in the Number group on the HOME tab.
   h. Save your work.

2. **Change font and font sizes.**
   a. Select the range of cells containing the column labels (in row 4).
   b. Change the font of the selection to Times New Roman.
   c. Increase the font size of the selection to 12 points.
   d. Increase the font size of the label in cell A1 to 14 points.
   e. Save your changes.

3. **Change font styles and alignment.**
   a. Apply the bold and italic font styles to the worksheet title in cell A1.
   b. Use the Merge & Center button to center the Life Insurance Premiums label over columns A through C.
   c. Apply the italic font style to the Life Insurance Premiums label.
   d. Add the bold font style to the labels in row 4.
   e. Use the Format Painter to copy the format in cell A4 to the range A5:A10.
   f. Apply the format in cell C10 to cell B14.
   g. Change the alignment of cell A10 to Align Right using a button in the Alignment group.

# Skills Review (continued)

**h.** Select the range of cells containing the column labels, then center them.

**i.** Remove the italic font style from the Life Insurance Premiums label, then increase the font size to 14.

**j.** Move the Life Insurance Premiums label to cell A3, then add the bold and underline font styles.

**k.** Save your changes.

**4. Adjust the column width.**

**a.** Resize column C to a width of 10.71 characters.

**b.** Use the AutoFit feature to resize columns A and B.

**c.** Clear the contents of cell A13 (do not delete the cell).

**d.** Change the text in cell A14 to **Monthly Premium**, then change the width of the column to 25 characters.

**e.** Save your changes.

**5. Insert and delete rows and columns.**

**a.** Insert a new row between rows 5 and 6.

**b.** Add a new department, **Charity**, in the newly inserted row. Enter **6** as the number of employees in the department.

**c.** Copy the formula in cell C7 to C6.

**d.** Add the following comment to cell A6: **New department**. Display the comment, then drag to move it out of the way, if necessary.

**e.** Add a new column between the Department and Employees columns with the title **Family Coverage**, then resize the column using AutoFit.

**f.** Delete the Legal row from the worksheet.

**g.** Move the value in cell C14 to cell B14.

**h.** Save your changes.

**6. Apply colors, patterns, and borders.**

**a.** Add Outside Borders around the range A4:D10.

**b.** Add a Bottom Double Border to cells C9 and D9 (above the calculated employee and premium totals).

**c.** Apply the Aqua, Accent 5, Lighter 80% fill color to the labels in the Department column (do not include the Total label).

**d.** Apply the Orange, Accent 6, Lighter 60% fill color to the range A4:D4.

**e.** Change the color of the font in the range A4:D4 to Red, Accent 2, Darker 25%.

**f.** Add a 12.5% Gray pattern style to cell A1.

**g.** Format the range A14:B14 with a fill color of Dark Blue, Text 2, Lighter 40%, change the font color to White, Background 1, then apply the bold font style.

**h.** Save your changes.

**7. Apply conditional formatting.**

**a.** Select the range D5:D9, then create a conditional format that changes cell contents to green fill with dark green text if the value is between 150 and 275.

**b.** Select the range C5:C9, then create a conditional format that changes cell contents to red text if the number of employees exceeds 10.

**c.** Apply a purple gradient-filled data bar to the range C5:C9. (*Hint*: Click Purple Data Bar in the Gradient Fill section.)

**d.** Use the Rules Manager to modify the conditional format in cells C5:C9 to display values greater than 10 in bold dark red text.

**e.** Merge and center the title (cell A1) over columns A through D.

**f.** Save your changes.

**8. Rename and move a worksheet.**

**a.** Name the Sheet1 tab **Insurance Data**.

**b.** Add a sheet to the workbook, then name the new sheet **Employee Data**.

**c.** Change the Insurance Data tab color to Red, Accent 2, Lighter 40%.

# Skills Review (continued)

  **d.** Change the Employee Data tab color to Aqua, Accent 5, Lighter 40%.

  **e.** Move the Employee Data sheet so it comes before (to the left of) the Insurance Data sheet.

  **f.** Make the Insurance Data sheet active, enter your name in cell A20, then save your work.

**9. Check spelling.**

  **a.** Move the cell pointer to cell A1.

  **b.** Use the Find & Select feature to replace the Accounting label in cell A5 with Accounting/Legal.

  **c.** Check the spelling in the worksheet using the spell checker, and correct any spelling errors if necessary.

  **d.** Save your changes, then compare your Insurance Data sheet to **FIGURE C-28**.

  **e.** Preview the Insurance Data sheet in Backstage view, submit your work to your instructor as directed, then close the workbook and exit Excel.

**FIGURE C-28**

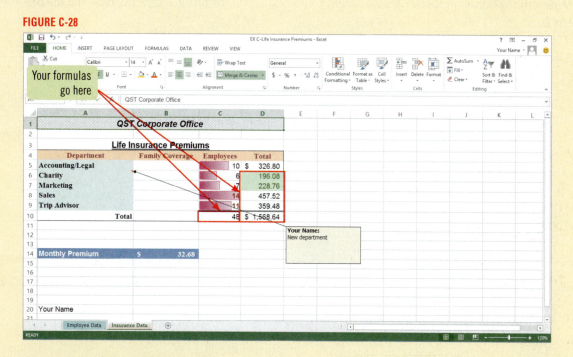

# Independent Challenge 1

You run a freelance accounting business, and one of your newest clients is Pen & Paper, a small office supply store. Now that you've converted the store's accounting records to Excel, the manager would like you to work on an analysis of the inventory. Although more items will be added later, the worksheet has enough items for you to begin your modifications.

  **a.** Start Excel, open the file EX C-3.xlsx from the location where you store your Data Files, then save it as **EX C-Pen & Paper Office Supply Inventory**.

  **b.** Create a formula in cell E4 that calculates the value of the items in stock based on the price paid per item in cell B4. Format the cell in the Comma Style.

  **c.** In cell F4, calculate the sale price of the items in stock using an absolute reference to the markup value shown in cell H1.

  **d.** Copy the formulas created above into the range E5:F14; first convert any necessary cell references to absolute so that the formulas work correctly.

  **e.** Apply bold to the column labels, and italicize the inventory items in column A.

  **f.** Make sure all columns are wide enough to display the data and labels.

  **g.** Format the values in the Sale Price column as Accounting number format with two decimal places.

  **h.** Format the values in the Price Paid column as Comma Style with two decimal places.

# Independent Challenge 1 (continued)

i. Add a row under #2 Pencils for **Digital cordless telephones**, price paid **53.45**, sold individually (**each**), with **23** on hand. Copy the appropriate formulas to cells E7:F7.

j. Verify that all the data in the worksheet is visible and formulas are correct. Adjust any items as needed, and check the spelling of the entire worksheet.

k. Use conditional formatting to apply yellow fill with dark yellow text to items with a quantity of less than 25 on hand.

l. Use an icon set of your choosing in the range D4:D15 to illustrate the relative differences between values in the range.

m. Add an outside border around the data in the Item column (*do not* include the Item column label).

n. Delete the row containing the Thumb tacks entry.

o. Enter your name in an empty cell below the data, then save the file. Compare your worksheet to the sample in **FIGURE C-29**.

p. Preview the worksheet in Backstage view, submit your work to your instructor as directed, close the workbook, then exit Excel.

FIGURE C-29

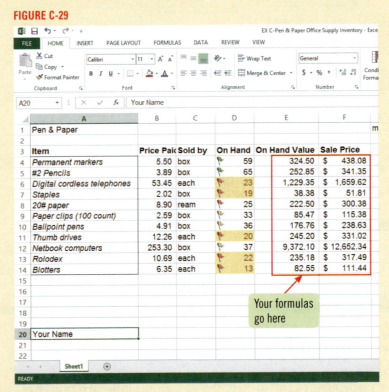

# Independent Challenge 2

You volunteer several hours each week with the Assistance League of San Antonio, and you are in charge of maintaining the membership list. You're currently planning a mailing campaign to members in certain regions of the city. You also want to create renewal letters for members whose membership expires soon. You decide to format the list to enhance the appearance of the worksheet and make your upcoming tasks easier to plan.

a. Start Excel, open the file EX C-4.xlsx from the location where you store your Data Files, then save it as **EX C-San Antonio Assistance League**.

b. Remove any blank columns.

c. Create a conditional format in the Zip Code column so that entries greater than 78249 appear in light red fill with dark red text.

d. Make all columns wide enough to fit their data and labels. (*Hint*: You can use any method to size the columns.)

e. Use formatting enhancements, such as fonts, font sizes, font styles, and fill colors, to make the worksheet more attractive.

# Independent Challenge 2 (continued)

f.  Center the column labels.

g.  Use conditional formatting so that entries for Year of Membership Expiration that are between 2017 and 2019 appear in green fill with bold black text. (*Hint*: Create a custom format for cells that meet the condition.)

h.  Adjust any items as necessary, then check the spelling.

i.  Change the name of the Sheet1 tab to one that reflects the sheet's contents, then add a tab color of your choice.

j.  Enter your name in an empty cell, then save your work.

k.  Preview the worksheet in Backstage view, make any final changes you think necessary, then submit your work to your instructor as directed. Compare your work to the sample shown in **FIGURE C-30**.

l.  Close the workbook, then exit Excel.

**FIGURE C-30**

| Member | Zip Code | Number of Employees | Year of Membership Expiration | Code | Year 2016 |
|---|---|---|---|---|---|
| Candy's Candy Shop | 78256 | 23 | 2020 | 3 | |
| Chip Technology | 78251 | 175 | 2021 | 3 | |
| Computer Attic | 78263 | 14 | 2018 | 2 | |
| Deluxe Auto Shop | 78245 | 17 | 2017 | 1 | |
| Dental Associates | 78287 | 15 | 2018 | 5 | |
| Dr. Mary Terese | 78263 | 12 | 2021 | 2 | |
| Dunkin' Donuts | 78278 | 10 | 2018 | 4 | |
| Earl's Restaurant | 78235 | 45 | 2019 | 3 | |
| First Federal Bank | 78267 | 36 | 2021 | 3 | |
| Friendly Chevy | 78286 | 17 | 2023 | 3 | |
| From Office | 78211 | 25 | 2022 | 5 | |
| General Hospital | 78225 | 538 | 2020 | 4 | |
| Grande Table | 78246 | 31 | 2019 | 4 | |
| Holiday Inn | 78221 | 75 | 2018 | 4 | |
| Ken's Florist Shop | 78241 | 10 | 2017 | 2 | |
| Lisa's Photo Studio | 78202 | 5 | 2020 | 4 | |
| Meineke Muffler | 78256 | 24 | 2019 | 1 | |
| Midas Muffler | 78221 | 22 | 2023 | 3 | |
| Mill Shoppe | 78205 | 165 | 2020 | 2 | |

# Independent Challenge 3

Prestige Press is a Boston-based publisher that manufactures children's books. As the finance manager for the company, one of your responsibilities is to analyze the monthly reports from the five district sales offices. Your boss, Joanne Bennington, has just asked you to prepare a quarterly sales report for an upcoming meeting. Because several top executives will be attending this meeting, Joanne reminds you that the report must look professional. In particular, she asks you to emphasize the company's surge in profits during the last month and to highlight the fact that the Northeastern district continues to outpace the other districts.

a.  Plan a worksheet that shows the company's sales during the first quarter. Assume that all books are the same price. Make sure you include the following:

  • The number of books sold (units sold) and the associated revenues (total sales) for each of the five district sales offices. The five sales districts are Northeastern, Midwestern, Southeastern, Southern, and Western.
  • Calculations that show month-by-month totals for January, February, and March, and a 3-month cumulative total.
  • Calculations that show each district's share of sales (percent of Total Sales).
  • Labels that reflect the month-by-month data as well as the cumulative data.
  • Formatting enhancements such as data bars that emphasize the recent month's sales surge and the Northeastern district's sales leadership.

b.  Ask yourself the following questions about the organization and formatting of the worksheet: What worksheet title and labels do you need, and where should they appear? How can you calculate the totals? What formulas can you copy to save time and keystrokes? Do any of these formulas need to use an absolute reference? How do you show dollar amounts? What information should be shown in bold? Do you need to use more than one font? Should you use more than one point size?

c.  Start Excel, then save a new, blank workbook as **EX C-Prestige Press** to the location where you store your Data Files.

# Independent Challenge 3 (continued)

**d.** Build the worksheet with your own price and sales data. Enter the titles and labels first, then enter the numbers and formulas. You can use the information in **TABLE C-4** to get started.

**TABLE C-4**

| Prestige Press | | | | | | | | | | | |
|---|---|---|---|---|---|---|---|---|---|---|---|
| 1st Quarter Sales Report | | | | | | | | | | | |
| | | | | | | | | | | | |
| | | January | | February | | March | | Total | | | |
| Office | Price | Units Sold | Sales | Units Sold | Sales | Units Sold | Sales | Units Sold | Sales | Total % of Sales | |
| Northeastern | | | | | | | | | | | |
| Midwestern | | | | | | | | | | | |
| Southeastern | | | | | | | | | | | |
| Southern | | | | | | | | | | | |
| Western | | | | | | | | | | | |

© 2014 Cengage Learning

**e.** Add a row beneath the data containing the totals for each column.

**f.** Adjust the column widths as necessary.

**g.** Change the height of row 1 to 33 points.

**h.** Format labels and values to enhance the look of the worksheet, and change the font styles and alignment if necessary.

**i.** Resize columns and adjust the formatting as necessary.

**j.** Add data bars for the monthly Units Sold columns.

**k.** Add a column that calculates a 25% increase in total sales dollars. Use an absolute cell reference in this calculation. (*Hint*: Make sure the current formatting is applied to the new information.)

**l.** Delete the contents of cells J4:K4 if necessary, then merge and center cell I4 over column I:K.

**m.** Add a bottom double border to cells I10:L10.

**n.** Enter your name in an empty cell.

**o.** Check the spelling in the workbook, change to a landscape orientation, save your work, then compare your work to **FIGURE C-31**.

**p.** Preview the worksheet in Backstage view, then submit your work to your instructor as directed.

**q.** Close the workbook file, then exit Excel.

**FIGURE C-31**

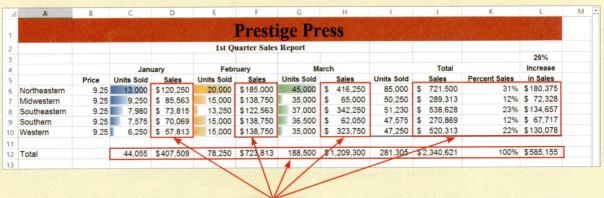

Formatting a Worksheet

# Independent Challenge 4: Explore

**This Independent Challenge requires an Internet connection.**

You are saving money to take the international trip you have always dreamed about. You plan to visit seven different countries over the course of 2 months, and you have budgeted an identical spending allowance in each country. You want to create a worksheet that calculates the amount of native currency you will have in each country based on the budgeted amount. You want the workbook to reflect the currency information for each country.

**a.** Start Excel, then save a new, blank workbook as **EX C-World Tour Budget** to the location where you store your Data Files.

**b.** Add a title at the top of the worksheet.

**c.** Think of seven countries you would like to visit, then enter column and row labels for your worksheet. (*Hint*: You may wish to include row labels for each country, plus column labels for the country, the $1 equivalent in native currency, the total amount of native currency you'll have in each country, and the name of each country's monetary unit.)

**d.** Decide how much money you want to bring to each country (for example, $1,000), and enter that in the worksheet.

**e.** Use your favorite search engine to find your own information sources on currency conversions for the countries you plan to visit.

**f.** Enter the cash equivalent to $1 in U.S. dollars for each country in your list.

**g.** Create an equation that calculates the amount of native currency you will have in each country, using an absolute cell reference in the formula.

**h.** Format the entries in the column containing the native currency $1 equivalent as Number number format with three decimal places, and format the column containing the total native currency budget with two decimal places, using the correct currency number format for each country. (*Hint*: Use the Number tab in the Format cells dialog box; choose the appropriate currency number format from the Symbol list.)

**i.** Create a conditional format that changes the font style and color of the calculated amount in the $1,000 US column to light red fill with dark red text if the amount exceeds **1000** units of the local currency.

**j.** Merge and center the worksheet title over the column headings.

**k.** Add any formatting you want to the column headings, and resize the columns as necessary.

**l.** Add a background color to the title and change the font color if you choose.

**m.** Enter your name in the header of the worksheet.

**n.** Spell check the worksheet, save your changes, compare your work to FIGURE C-32, then preview the worksheet in Backstage view, and submit your work to your instructor as directed.

**o.** Close the workbook and exit Excel.

FIGURE C-32

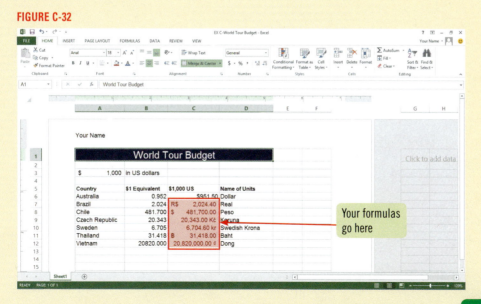

# Visual Workshop

Open the file EX C-5.xlsx from the location where you store your Data Files, then save it as **EX C-Tip-Top Temps**. Use the skills you learned in this unit to format the worksheet so it looks like the one shown in FIGURE C-33. Create a conditional format in the Level column so that entries greater than 3 appear in light red fill with dark red text. Create an additional conditional format in the Review Cycle column so that any value equal to 3 appears in black fill with white bold text.

Replace the Accounting department label with **Legal**. (*Hint:* The only additional font used in this exercise is 18-point Times New Roman in row 1.) Enter your name in the upper-right part of the header, check the spelling in the worksheet, save your changes, then submit your work to your instructor as directed. (*Hint:* Zoom out until the Zoom level is 100%.)

**FIGURE C-33**

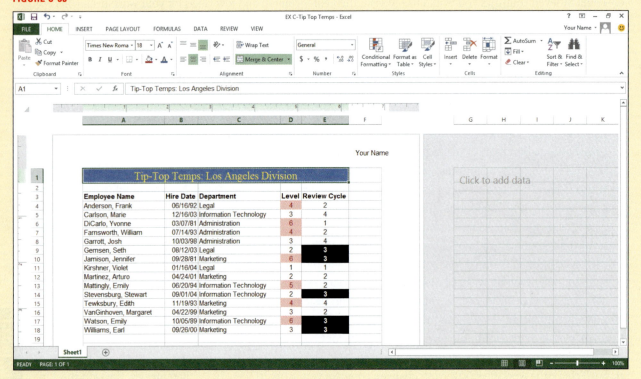

# Working with Charts

**CASE** ▶ At the upcoming annual meeting, Grace Wong wants to emphasize spending patterns at Quest Specialty Travel. She asks you to create a chart showing the trends in company expenses over the past four quarters.

## Unit Objectives

After completing this unit, you will be able to:

- Plan a chart
- Create a chart
- Move and resize a chart
- Change the chart design
- Change the chart format
- Format a chart
- Annotate and draw on a chart
- Create a pie chart

## Files You Will Need

| | |
|---|---|
| EX D-1.xlsx | EX D-4.xlsx |
| EX D-2.xlsx | EX D-5.xlsx |
| EX D-3.xlsx | EX D-6.xlsx |

# Create a Chart

Learning
Outcomes
• Create a chart
• Switch a chart's
  columns/rows
• Add a chart title

To create a chart in Excel, you first select the range in a worksheet containing the data you want to chart. Once you've selected a range, you can use buttons on the INSERT tab on the Ribbon to create a chart based on the data in the range. **CASE** ▶ *Using the worksheet containing the quarterly expense data, you create a chart that shows how the expenses in each country varied across the quarters.*

## STEPS

**QUICK TIP**

When charting data for a particular time period, make sure all series are for the same time period.

1. **Start Excel, open the file EX D-1.xlsx from the location where you store your Data Files, then save it as EX D-Quarterly Tour Expenses**

   You want the chart to include the quarterly tour expenses values, as well as quarter and country labels. You don't include the Total column and row because the figures in these cells would skew the chart.

2. **Select the range A4:E12, then click the Quick Analysis tool 📊 in the lower-right corner of the range**

   The Quick Analysis tool contains a tab that lets you quickly insert commonly used charts. The CHARTS tab includes buttons for each major chart type, plus a More Charts button for additional chart types, such as stock charts for charting stock market data.

**QUICK TIP**

To base a chart on data in nonadjacent ranges, press and hold [Ctrl] while selecting each range, then use the INSERT tab to create the chart.

3. **Click the CHARTS tab, verify that the Clustered Column is selected, as shown in FIGURE D-3, then click Clustered Column**

   The chart is inserted in the center of the worksheet, and two contextual CHART TOOLS tabs appear on the Ribbon: DESIGN, and FORMAT. On the DESIGN tab, which is currently in front, you can quickly change the chart type, chart layout, and chart style, and you can swap how the columns and rows of data in the worksheet are represented in the chart. When seen in the Normal view, three tools display to the right of the chart: these enable you to add, remove, or change chart elements ➕, set a style and color scheme 🖌, and filter the results shown in a chart 🔽. Currently, the countries are charted along the horizontal x-axis, with the quarterly expense dollar amounts charted along the y-axis. This lets you easily compare the quarterly expenses for each country.

4. **Click the Switch Row/Column button in the Data group on the CHART TOOLS DESIGN tab**

   The quarters are now charted along the x-axis. The expense amounts per country are charted along the y-axis, as indicated by the updated legend. See **FIGURE D-4**.

5. **Click the Undo button ↩ on the Quick Access toolbar**

   The chart returns to its original design.

**QUICK TIP**

You can also triple-click to select the chart title text.

6. **Click the Chart Title placeholder to show the text box, click anywhere in the Chart Title text box, press [Ctrl][A] to select the text, type Quarterly Tour Expenses, then click anywhere in the chart to deselect the title**

   Adding a title helps identify the chart. The border around the chart and the chart's **sizing handles**, the small series of dots at the corners and sides of the chart's border, indicate that the chart is selected. See **FIGURE D-5**. Your chart might be in a different location on the worksheet and may look slightly different; you will move and resize it in the next lesson. Any time a chart is selected, as it is now, a blue border surrounds the worksheet data range on which the chart is based, a purple border surrounds the cells containing the category axis labels, and a red border surrounds the cells containing the data series labels. This chart is known as an **embedded chart** because it is inserted directly in the current worksheet and doesn't exist in a separate file. Embedding a chart in the current sheet is the default selection when creating a chart, but you can also embed a chart on a different sheet in the workbook, or on a newly created chart sheet. A **chart sheet** is a sheet in a workbook that contains only a chart that is linked to the workbook data.

7. **Save your work**

Working with Charts

**FIGURE D-3:** CHARTS tab in Quick Analysis tool

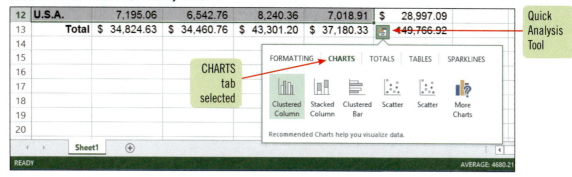

**FIGURE D-4:** Clustered Column chart with different presentation of data

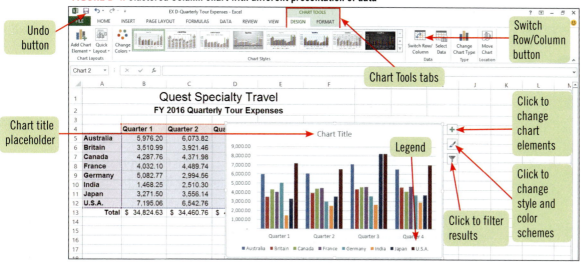

**FIGURE D-5:** Chart with rows and columns restored and title added

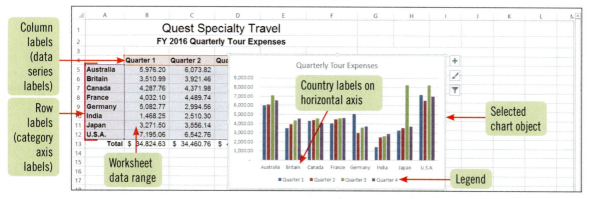

Excel 2013

## Creating sparklines

You can quickly create a miniature chart called a **sparkline** that serves as a visual indicator of data trends. You can create a sparkline by selecting a range of data, clicking the Quick Analysis tool, clicking the SPARKLINES tab, then clicking the type of sparkline you want. (The sparkline appears in the cell immediately adjacent to the selected range.) You can also select a range, click the INSERT tab, then click the Line, Column, or Win/Loss button in the Sparklines group. In the Create Sparklines dialog box that opens, enter the cell in which you want the sparkline to appear, then click OK.

**FIGURE D-6** shows a sparkline created in a cell. Any changes to data in the range are reflected in the sparkline. To delete a selected sparkline from a cell, click the Clear button in the Group group on the SPARKLINE TOOLS DESIGN tab.

**FIGURE D-6:** Sparkline in a cell

# Move and Resize a Chart

**Learning Outcomes**
• Reposition a chart
• Resize a chart
• Modify a legend
• Modify chart data

A chart is an **object**, or an independent element on a worksheet, and is not located in a specific cell or range. You can select an object by clicking it; sizing handles around the object indicate it is selected. (When a chart is selected in Excel, the Name box, which normally tells you the address of the active cell, tells you the chart number.) You can move a selected chart anywhere on a worksheet without affecting formulas or data in the worksheet. Any data changed in the worksheet is automatically updated in the chart. You can even move a chart to a different sheet in the workbook and it will still reflect the original data. You can resize a chart to improve its appearance by dragging its sizing handles. You can reposition chart objects (such as a title or legend) to predefined locations using commands using the Chart Elements button or the Add Chart Element button on the CHART TOOLS DESIGN tab, or you can freely move any chart object by dragging it or by cutting and pasting it to a new location. When you point to a chart object, the name of the object appears as a ScreenTip. **CASE** ▶ *You want to resize the chart, position it below the worksheet data, and move the legend.*

## STEPS

**QUICK TIP**
To delete a selected chart, press [Delete].

1. **Make sure the chart is still selected, then position the pointer over the chart**

   The pointer shape ✛ indicates that you can move the chart. For a table of commonly used object pointers, refer to **TABLE D-2**.

**TROUBLE**
If you do not drag a blank area on the chart, you might inadvertently move a chart element instead of the whole chart; if this happens, undo the action and try again.

2. **Position ✛ on a blank area near the upper-left edge of the chart, press and hold the left mouse button, drag the chart until its upper-left corner is at the upper-left corner of cell A16, then release the mouse button**

   As you drag the chart, you can see the chart being dragged. When you release the mouse button, the chart appears in the new location.

3. **Scroll down so you can see the whole chart, position the pointer on the right-middle sizing handle until it changes to ↔, then drag the right border of the chart to the right edge of column G**

   The chart is widened. See **FIGURE D-7**.

**QUICK TIP**
To resize a selected chart to an exact specification, click the CHART TOOLS FORMAT tab, then enter the desired height and width in the Size group.

4. **Position the pointer over the upper-middle sizing handle until it changes to ↕, then drag the top border of the chart to the top edge of row 15**

5. **Position the pointer over the lower-middle sizing handle until it changes to ↕, then drag the bottom border of the chart to the bottom border of row 26**

   You can move any object on a chart. You want to align the top of the legend with the top of the plot area.

**QUICK TIP**
You can move a legend to the right, top, left, or bottom of a chart by clicking Legend in the Add Chart Element button in the Chart Layouts group on the CHART TOOLS DESIGN tab, then clicking a location option.

6. **Click the Quick Layout button in the Chart Layouts group of the CHART TOOLS DESIGN tab, click Layout 1 (in the upper-left corner of the palette), click the legend to select it, press and hold [Shift], drag the legend up using ✛ so the dotted outline is approximately 1/4" above the top of the plot area, then release [Shift]**

   When you click the legend, sizing handles appear around it and "Legend" appears as a ScreenTip when the pointer hovers over the object. As you drag, a dotted outline of the legend border appears. Pressing and holding the [Shift] key holds the horizontal position of the legend as you move it vertically. Although the sizing handles on objects within a chart look different from the sizing handles that surround a chart, they function the same way.

7. **Click cell A12, type United States, click the Enter button ✓ on the formula bar, use AutoFit to resize column A, then save your work**

   The axis label changes to reflect the updated cell contents, as shown in **FIGURE D-8**. Changing any data in the worksheet modifies corresponding text or values in the chart. Because the chart is no longer selected, the CHART TOOLS tabs no longer appear on the Ribbon.

Working with Charts

**FIGURE D-7:** Moved and resized chart

**FIGURE D-8:** Worksheet with modified legend and label

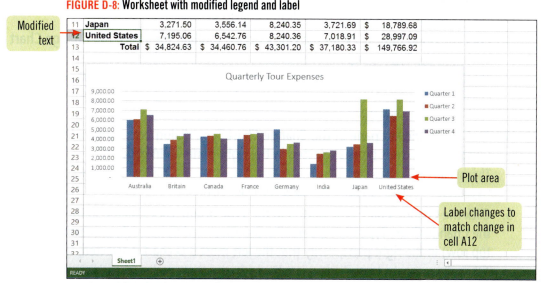

**TABLE D-2:** Common object pointers

| name | pointer | use | name | pointer | use |
|------|---------|-----|------|---------|-----|
| Diagonal resizing | ⤢ or ⤡ | Change chart shape from corners | I-beam | I | Edit object text |
| Draw | + | Draw an object | Move | ✛ | Move object |
| Horizontal resizing | ⟷ | Change object width | Vertical resizing | ↕ | Change object height |

## Moving an embedded chart to a sheet

Suppose you have created an embedded chart that you decide would look better on a chart sheet or in a different worksheet. You can make this change without recreating the entire chart. To do so, first select the chart, click the CHART TOOLS DESIGN tab, then click the Move Chart button in the Location group. The Move Chart dialog box opens. To move the chart to its own chart sheet, click the New sheet option button, type a name for the new sheet if desired, then click OK. If the chart is already on its own sheet, click the Object in option button, select the worksheet to where you want to move it, then click OK.

# Format a Chart

**Learning Outcomes**
• Change the fill of a data series
• Use Live Preview to see a new data series color
• Apply a style to a data series

Formatting a chart can make it easier to read and understand. Many formatting enhancements can be made using the CHART TOOLS FORMAT tab. You can change the fill color for a specific data series, or you can apply a shape style to a title or a data series using the Shape Styles group. Shape styles make it possible to apply multiple formats, such as an outline, fill color, and text color, all with a single click. You can also apply different fill colors, outlines, and effects to chart objects using arrows and buttons in the Shape Styles group. **CASE** *You want to use a different color for one data series in the chart and apply a shape style to another to enhance the look of the chart.*

## STEPS

1. **With the chart selected, click the CHART TOOLS FORMAT tab on the Ribbon, then click any column in the Quarter 4 data series**

   The CHART TOOLS FORMAT tab opens, and handles appear on each column in the Quarter 4 data series, indicating that the entire series is selected.

2. **Click the Shape Fill list arrow in the Shape Styles group on the CHART TOOLS FORMAT tab**

3. **Click Orange, Accent 6 (first row, 10th from the left) as shown in FIGURE D-15**

   All the columns for the series become orange, and the legend changes to match the new color. You can also change the color of selected objects by applying a shape style.

4. **Click any column in the Quarter 3 data series**

   Handles appear on each column in the Quarter 3 data series.

5. **Click the More button ⟱ on the Shape Styles gallery, then *hover the pointer* over the Moderate Effect – Olive Green, Accent 3 shape style (fifth row, fourth from the left) in the gallery, as shown in FIGURE D-16**

   Live Preview shows the data series in the chart with the shape style applied.

**QUICK TIP**
To apply a WordArt style to a text object (such as the chart title), select the object, then click a style in the WordArt Styles group on the CHART TOOLS FORMAT tab.

6. **Click the Subtle Effect – Olive Green, Accent 3 shape style (fourth row, fourth from the left) in the gallery**

   The style for the data series changes, as shown in FIGURE D-17.

7. **Save your work**

### Previewing a chart

To print or preview just a chart, select the chart (or make the chart sheet active), click the FILE tab, then click Print on the navigation bar. To reposition a chart by changing the page's margins, click the Show Margins button ▦ in the lower-right corner of the Print tab to display the margins in the preview. You can drag the margin lines to the exact settings you want; as the margins change, the size and placement of the chart on the page changes too.

**FIGURE D-15:** New shape fill applied to data series

**FIGURE D-16:** Live Preview of new style applied to data series

**FIGURE D-17:** Style of data series changed

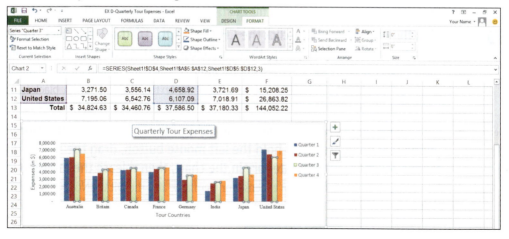

## Changing alignment and angle in axis labels and titles

The buttons on the CHART TOOLS DESIGN tab provide a few options for positioning axis labels and titles, but you can customize their position and rotation to exact specifications using the Format Axis pane or Format Axis Title pane. With a chart selected, right-click the axis text you want to modify, then click Format Axis or Format Axis Title on the shortcut menu. In the pane that is displayed, click the Size & Properties button, then select the appropriate Text layout option. You can also create a custom angle by clicking the Custom angle up and down arrows. When you have made the desired changes, close the pane.

# Practice

Put your skills into practice with **SAM Projects!** SAM Projects for this unit can be found online. If you have a SAM account, go to www.cengage.com/sam2013 to download the most recent Project Instruction and Start Files.

## Concepts Review

**Label each element of the Excel chart shown in FIGURE D-25.**

**FIGURE D-25**

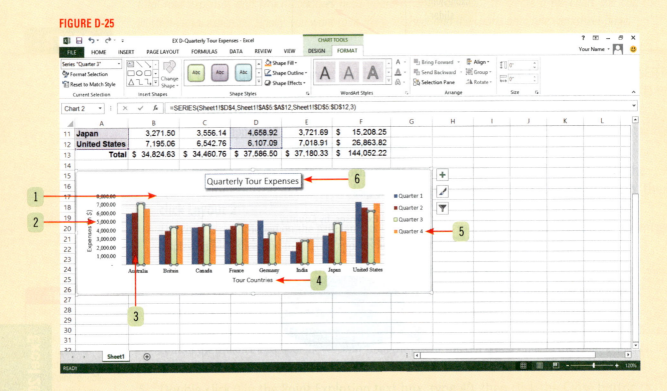

**Match each chart type with the statement that best describes it.**

7. Area
8. Line
9. Column
10. Combination
11. Pie

a. Displays a column and line chart using different scales of measurement
b. Compares trends over even time intervals
c. Compares data using columns
d. Compares data as parts of a whole
e. Shows how volume changes over time

**Select the best answer from the list of choices.**

12. **Which tab appears only when a chart is selected?**
    a. INSERT
    b. CHART TOOLS FORMAT
    c. REVIEW
    d. PAGE LAYOUT

13. **Which is *not* an example of a SmartArt graphic?**
    a. Sparkline
    b. Basic Matrix
    c. Organization Chart
    d. Basic Pyramid

14. **How do you move an embedded chart to a chart sheet?**
    a. Click a button on the CHART TOOLS DESIGN tab.
    b. Drag the chart to the sheet tab.
    c. Delete the chart, switch to a different sheet, then create a new chart.
    d. Use the Copy and Paste buttons on the Ribbon.

15. **The object in a chart that identifies the colors used for each data series is a(n):**
    a. Data marker.
    b. Data point.
    c. Organizer.
    d. Legend.

16. **A collection of related data points in a chart is called a:**
    a. Data series.
    b. Data tick.
    c. Cell address.
    d. Value title.

17. **Which tab on the Ribbon do you use to create a chart?**
    a. DESIGN
    b. INSERT
    c. PAGE LAYOUT
    d. FORMAT

# Skills Review

1. **Plan a chart.**
   a. Start Excel, open the Data File EX D-2.xlsx from the location where you store your Data Files, then save it as **EX D-Departmental Software Usage**.
   b. Describe the type of chart you would use to plot this data.
   c. What chart type would you use to compare the number of Excel users in each department?

2. **Create a chart.**
   a. In the worksheet, select the range containing all the data and headings.
   b. Click the Quick Analysis tool.
   c. Create a Clustered Column chart, then add the chart title **Software Usage, by Department** above the chart.
   d. If necessary, click the Switch Row/Column button so the Department appears as the x-axis.
   e. Save your work.

# Independent Challenge 1

You are the operations manager for the Tulsa Arts Alliance in Oklahoma. Each year the group applies to various state and federal agencies for matching funds. For this year's funding proposal, you need to create charts to document the number of productions in previous years.

**a.** Start Excel, open the file EX D-3.xlsx from the location where you store your Data Files, then save it as **EX D-Tulsa Arts Alliance**.

**b.** Take some time to plan your charts. Which type of chart or charts might best illustrate the information you need to display? What kind of chart enhancements do you want to use? Will a 3-D effect make your chart easier to understand?

**c.** Create a Clustered Column chart for the data.

**d.** Change at least one of the colors used in a data series.

**e.** Make the appropriate modifications to the chart to make it visually attractive and easier to read and understand. Include a legend to the right of the chart, and add chart titles and horizontal and vertical axis titles using the text shown in **TABLE D-3**.

**TABLE D-3**

| title | text |
|---|---|
| Chart title | Tulsa Arts Alliance Events |
| Vertical axis title | Number of Events |
| Horizontal axis title | Types of Events |

© 2014 Cengage Learning

**f.** Create at least two additional charts for the same data to show how different chart types display the same data. Reposition each new chart so that all charts are visible in the worksheet. One of the additional charts should be a pie chart; the other is up to you.

**g.** Modify each new chart as necessary to improve its appearance and effectiveness. A sample worksheet containing three charts based on the worksheet data is shown in **FIGURE D-27**.

**h.** Enter your name in the worksheet header.

**i.** Save your work. Before printing, preview the worksheet in Backstage view, then adjust any settings as necessary so that all the worksheet data and charts print on a single page.

**j.** Submit your work to your instructor as directed.

**k.** Close the workbook, then exit Excel.

**FIGURE D-27**

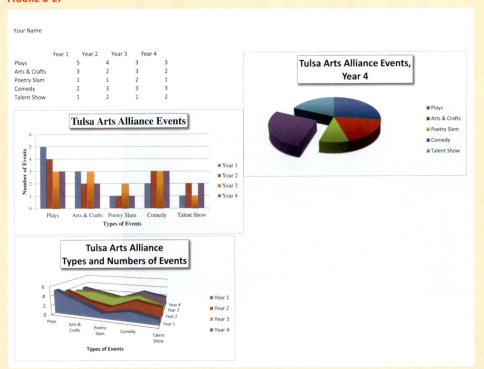

# Independent Challenge 2

You work at Bark Bark Bark, a locally owned day spa for dogs. One of your responsibilities at the day spa is to manage the company's sales and expenses using Excel. Another is to convince the current staff that Excel can help them make daily operating decisions more easily and efficiently. To do this, you've decided to create charts using the previous year's operating expenses including rent, utilities, and payroll. The manager will use these charts at the next monthly meeting.

**a.** Start Excel, open the Data File EX D-4.xlsx from the location where you store your Data Files, then save it as **EX D-Bark Bark Bark Doggie Day Spa Analysis**.

**b.** Decide which data in the worksheet should be charted. What chart types are best suited for the information you need to show? What kinds of chart enhancements are necessary?

**c.** Create a 3-D Clustered Column chart in the worksheet showing the expense data for all four quarters. (*Hint*: The expense categories should appear on the x-axis. Do not include the totals.)

**d.** Change the vertical axis labels (Expenses data) so that no decimals are displayed. (*Hint*: Right-click the axis labels you want to modify, click Format Axis, click the Number category in the Format Axis pane, change the number of decimal places, then close the Format Axis pane.)

**e.** Using the sales data, create two charts on this worksheet that compare the sales amounts. (*Hint*: Move each chart to a new location on the worksheet, then deselect it before creating the next one.)

**f.** In one chart of the sales data, add data labels, then add chart titles as you see fit.

**g.** Make any necessary formatting changes to make the charts look more attractive, then enter your name in a worksheet cell.

**h.** Save your work.

**i.** Preview each chart in Backstage view, and adjust any items as needed. Fit the worksheet to a single page, then submit your work to your instructor as directed. A sample of a printed worksheet is shown in FIGURE D-28.

**j.** Close the workbook, then exit Excel.

**FIGURE D-28**

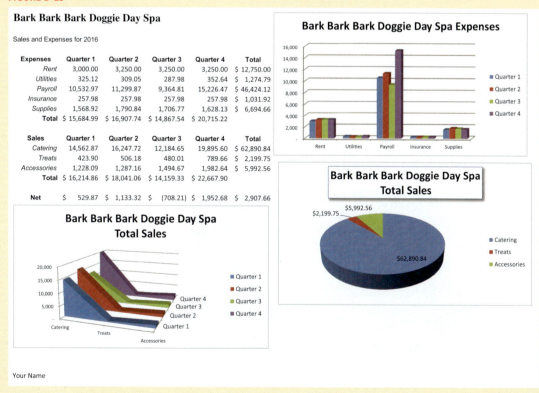

# Independent Challenge 3

You are working as an account representative at a magazine called *Creativity*. You have been examining the expenses incurred recently. The CEO wants to examine expenses designed to increase circulation and has asked you to prepare charts that can be used in this evaluation. In particular, you want to see how dollar amounts compare among the different expenses, and you also want to see how expenses compare with each other proportional to the total budget.

a. Start Excel, open the Data File EX D-5.xlsx from the location where you store your Data Files, then save it as **EX D-Creativity Magazine**.

b. Identify three types of charts that seem best suited to illustrate the data in the range A16:B24. What kinds of chart enhancements are necessary?

c. Create at least two different types of charts that show the distribution of circulation expenses. (*Hint*: Move each chart to a new location on the same worksheet.) One of the charts should be a 3-D pie chart.

d. In at least one of the charts, add annotated text and arrows highlighting important data, such as the largest expense.

e. Change the color of at least one data series in at least one of the charts.

f. Add chart titles and category and value axis titles where appropriate. Format the titles with a font of your choice. Apply a shadow to the chart title in at least one chart.

g. Add your name to a section of the header, then save your work.

h. Explode a slice from the 3-D pie chart.

i. Add a data label to the exploded pie slice.

j. Preview the worksheet in Backstage view. Adjust any items as needed. Be sure the charts are all visible on one page. Compare your work to the sample in FIGURE D-29.

k. Submit your work to your instructor as directed, close the workbook, then exit Excel.

## FIGURE D-29

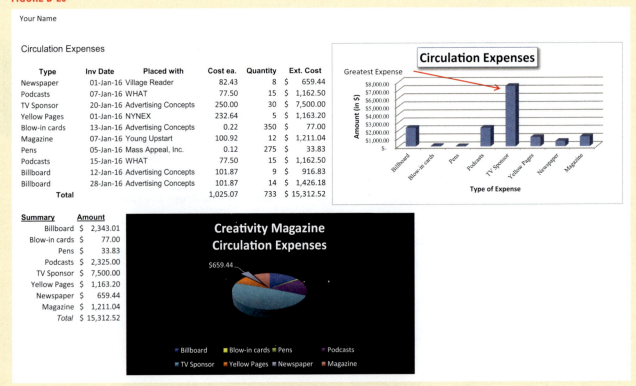

# Independent Challenge 4: Explore

**This Independent Challenge requires an Internet connection.**

A cash inheritance from a distant relative has finally been deposited in your bank account, and you have decided to purchase a home. You have a good idea where you'd like to live, and you decide to use the web to find out more about houses that are currently available.

a. Start Excel, then save a new, blank workbook as **EX D-My Dream House** to the location where you save your Data Files.

b. Decide on where you would like to live, and use your favorite search engine to find information sources on homes for sale in that area. (*Hint*: Try using realtor.com or other realtor-sponsored sites.)

c. Determine a price range and features within the home. Find data for at least five homes that meet your location and price requirements, and enter them in the worksheet. See **TABLE D-4** for a suggested data layout.

d. Format the data so it looks attractive and professional.

e. Create any type of column chart using only the House and Asking Price data. Place it on the same worksheet as the data. Include a descriptive title.

f. Change the colors in the chart using the chart style of your choice.

g. Enter your name in a section of the header.

h. Create an additional chart: a combo chart that plots the asking price on one axis and the size of the home on the other axis. (*Hint*: Use Help to get tips on how to chart with a secondary axis.)

i. Save the workbook. Preview the worksheet in Backstage view and make adjustments if necessary to fit all of the information on one page. See **FIGURE D-30** for an example of what your worksheet might look like.

j. Submit your work to your instructor as directed.

k. Close the workbook, then exit Excel.

**TABLE D-4**

| suggested data layout | | | | | |
|---|---|---|---|---|---|
| Location | | | | | |
| Price range | | | | | |
| | House 1 | House 2 | House 3 | House 4 | House 5 |
| Asking price | | | | | |
| Bedrooms | | | | | |
| Bathrooms | | | | | |
| Year built | | | | | |
| Size (in sq. ft.) | | | | | |

© 2014 Cengage Learning

**FIGURE D-30**

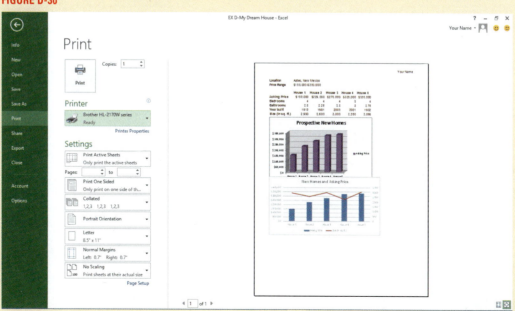

# Visual Workshop

Open the Data File EX D-6.xlsx from the location where you store your Data Files, then save it as **EX D-Projected Project Expenses**. Format the worksheet data so it looks like **FIGURE D-31**, then create and modify two charts to match the ones shown in the figure. You will need to make formatting, layout, and design changes once you create the charts. (*Hint*: The shadow used in the 3-D pie chart title is made using the Outer Offset Diagonal Top Right shadow.) Enter your name in the left text box of the header, then save and preview the worksheet. Submit your work to your instructor as directed, then close the workbook and exit Excel.

**FIGURE D-31**

Your Name

### Projected Project Expenses

| | Quarter 1 | Quarter 2 | Quarter 3 | Quarter 4 | Total |
|---|---|---|---|---|---|
| **Project 1** | 1,825.00 | 1,835.00 | 1,935.00 | 2,500.00 | 8,095 |
| **Project 2** | 2,700.00 | 2,490.00 | 2,400.00 | 2,150.00 | 9,740 |
| **Project 3** | 2,850.00 | 2,930.00 | 3,190.00 | 3,500.00 | 12,470 |
| **Project 4** | 1,572.00 | 1,720.00 | 1,550.00 | 1,710.00 | 6,552 |
| **Project 5** | 2,290.00 | 2,060.00 | 6,400.00 | 2,800.00 | 13,550 |
| **Project 6** | 2,890.00 | 3,550.00 | 3,735.00 | 3,440.00 | 13,615 |
| **Total** | 14,127 | 14,585 | 19,210 | 16,100 | |

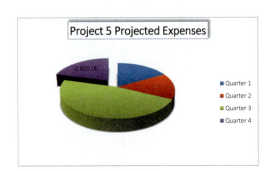

# Analyzing Data Using Formulas

**CASE** ▶ Kate Morgan, Quest's vice president of sales, uses Excel formulas and functions to analyze sales data for the U.S. region and to consolidate sales data from several worksheets. Because management is considering adding a new regional branch, Kate asks you to estimate the loan costs for a new office facility and to compare tour sales in the existing U.S. offices.

## Unit Objectives

After completing this unit, you will be able to:

- Format data using text functions
- Sum a data range based on conditions
- Consolidate data using a formula
- Check formulas for errors
- Construct formulas using named ranges

- Build a logical formula with the IF function
- Build a logical formula with the AND function
- Calculate payments with the PMT function

## Files You Will Need

EX E-1.xlsx    EX E-5.xlsx
EX E-2.xlsx    EX E-6.xlsx
EX E-3.xlsx    EX E-7.xlsx
EX E-4.xlsx

# Practice

## Concepts Review

**FIGURE E-21**

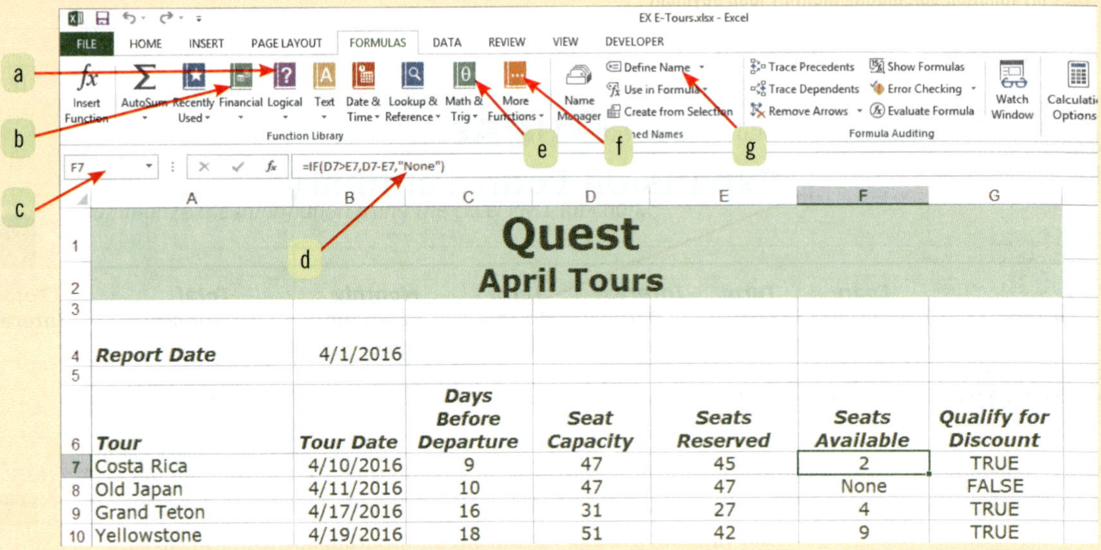

![Excel screenshot showing the Formulas ribbon tab with labeled callouts a, b, c, d, e, f, g pointing to various ribbon elements, and a worksheet titled "Quest April Tours". The formula bar shows =IF(D7>E7,D7-E7,"None") for cell F7.]

| Tour | Tour Date | Days Before Departure | Seat Capacity | Seats Reserved | Seats Available | Qualify for Discount |
|------|-----------|----------------------|---------------|----------------|-----------------|----------------------|
| Costa Rica | 4/10/2016 | 9 | 47 | 45 | 2 | TRUE |
| Old Japan | 4/11/2016 | 10 | 47 | 47 | None | FALSE |
| Grand Teton | 4/17/2016 | 16 | 31 | 27 | 4 | TRUE |
| Yellowstone | 4/19/2016 | 18 | 51 | 42 | 9 | TRUE |

Report Date: 4/1/2016

1. Which element do you click to add a statistical function to a worksheet?
2. Which element do you click to name a cell or range?
3. Which element points to the area where the name of a selected cell or range appears?
4. Which element points to a logical formula?
5. Which element do you click to insert a PMT function into a worksheet?
6. Which element do you click to add a SUMIF function to a worksheet?
7. Which element do you click to add an IF function to a worksheet?

## Match each term with the statement that best describes it.

8. PV
9. FV
10. PROPER
11. SUMIF
12. test_cond

a. Function used to change the first letter of a string to uppercase
b. Function used to determine the future amount of an investment
c. Part of the PMT function that represents the loan amount
d. Part of the IF function that the conditions are stated in
e. Function used to conditionally total cells

## Select the best answer from the list of choices.

13. When you enter the rate and nper arguments in a PMT function, you must:
    a. Be consistent in the units used.
    b. Multiply both units by 12.
    c. Divide both values by 12.
    d. Always use annual units.
14. To express conditions such as less than or equal to, you can use a:
    a. Text formula.
    b. Comparison operator.
    c. PMT function.
    d. Statistical function.

**15. Which of the following statements is false?**

a. When used in formulas, names become relative cell references by default.

b. Names cannot contain spaces.

c. Named ranges make formulas easier to build.

d. If you move a named cell or range, its name moves with it.

**16. Which of the following is an external reference indicator in a formula?**

a.   &                              c. !

b.   :                                  d. =

**17. When using text in logical tests, the text must be enclosed in:**

a.   " "                               c. !

b.   ( )                               d. < >

**18. Which function joins text strings into one text string?**

a. Proper                             c. Combine

b. Join                                d. Concatenate

# Skills Review

**1. Format data using text functions.**

a. Start Excel, open the file EX E-3.xlsx from the location where you store your Data Files, then save it as **EX E-Reviews**.

b. On the Managers worksheet, select cell B4 and use the Flash Fill button on the DATA tab to enter the names into column B.

c. In cell D2, enter the text formula to convert the first letter of the department in cell C2 to uppercase, then copy the formula in cell D2 into the range D3:D9.

d. In cell E2, enter the text formula to convert all letters of the department in cell C2 to uppercase, then copy the formula in cell E2 into the range E3:E9.

e. In cell F2, use the text formula to convert all letters of the department in cell C2 to lowercase, then copy the formula in cell F2 into the range F3:F9.

f. In cell G2, use the text formula to substitute "Human Resources" for "hr" if that text exists in cell F2. (*Hint*: In the Function Arguments dialog box, Text is F2, Old_text is "hr", and New_text is "Human Resources".) Copy the formula in cell G2 into the range G3:G9 to change the other cells containing "hr" to "Human Resources" and widen column G to fit the new entries. (The marketing and sales entries will not change because the formula searches for the text "hr".)

g. Save your work, then enter your name in the worksheet footer. Compare your screen to **FIGURE E-22**.

h. Display the formulas in the worksheet.

i. Redisplay the formula results.

**2. Sum a data range based on conditions.**

a. Make the HR sheet active.

b. In cell B20, use the COUNTIF function to count the number of employees with a rating of 5.

c. In cell B21, use the AVERAGEIF function to average the salaries of those with a rating of 5.

d. In cell B22, enter the SUMIF function that totals the salaries of employees with a rating of 5.

e. Format cells B21 and B22 with the Number format using commas and no decimals. Save your work, then compare your formula results to **FIGURE E-23**.

**FIGURE E-22**

| | A | B | C | D | E | F | G |
|---|---|---|---|---|---|---|---|
| 1 | | Name | Department | Proper | Upper | Lower | Substitute |
| 2 | JohnSmith@company.com | John Smith | hr | Hr | HR | hr | Human Resources |
| 3 | PaulaJones@company.com | Paula Jones | sALES | Sales | SALES | sales | sales |
| 4 | LindaKristol@company.com | Linda Kristol | MarKeting | Marketing | MARKETING | marketing | marketing |
| 5 | AlMeng@company.com | Al Meng | hR | Hr | HR | hr | Human Resources |
| 6 | RobertDelgado@company.com | Robert Delgado | saLEs | Sales | SALES | sales | sales |
| 7 | HarryDegual@company.com | Harry Degual | saleS | Sales | SALES | sales | sales |
| 8 | JodyWilliams@company.com | Jody Williams | hR | Hr | HR | hr | Human Resources |
| 9 | MaryAbbott@company.com | Mary Abbott | MaRketing | Marketing | MARKETING | marketing | marketing |
| 10 | | | | | | | |

**FIGURE E-23**

| | | |
|---|---|---|
| 17 | | |
| 18 | **Department Statistics** | |
| 19 | **Top Rating** | |
| 20 | Number | 5 |
| 21 | Average Salary | 31,200 |
| 22 | Total Salary | 156,000 |
| 23 | | |

# Visual Workshop

Open the file EX E-7.xlsx from the location where you store your Data Files, then save it as **EX E-Summary**. Create the worksheet shown in **FIGURE E-31** using the data in columns B, C, and D along with the following criteria:

- The employee is eligible for a bonus if:
  - The employee has sales that exceed the sales quota.
    **AND**
  - The employee has a performance rating of six or higher.
- If the employee is eligible for a bonus, the bonus amount is calculated as two percent of the sales amount. Otherwise the bonus amount is 0. (*Hint*: Use an AND formula to determine if a person is eligible for a bonus, and use an IF formula to check eligibility and to enter the bonus amount.) Enter your name in the worksheet footer, save the workbook, preview the worksheet, then submit the worksheet to your instructor.

**FIGURE E-31**

| | A | B | C | D | E | F | G |
|---|---|---|---|---|---|---|---|
| 1 | | | Westside Plumbing Supplies | | | | |
| 2 | | | Bonus Pay Summary | | | | |
| 3 | Last Name | Quota | Sales | Performance Rating | Eligible | Bonus Amount | |
| 4 | Adams | $135,000 | $157,557 | 7 | TRUE | $3,151 | |
| 5 | Gurano | $90,774 | $91,223 | 3 | FALSE | $0 | |
| 6 | Greely | $112,663 | $100,307 | 9 | FALSE | $0 | |
| 7 | Hanlon | $149,335 | $153,887 | 5 | FALSE | $0 | |
| 8 | Perez | $145,000 | $151,228 | 8 | TRUE | $3,025 | |
| 9 | Medway | $130,000 | $152,774 | 5 | FALSE | $0 | |
| 10 | Merkel | $152,885 | $160,224 | 7 | TRUE | $3,204 | |
| 11 | Star | $98,000 | $87,224 | 3 | FALSE | $0 | |
| 12 | Gonzalez | $90,000 | $86,700 | 9 | FALSE | $0 | |
| 13 | | | | | | | |
| 14 | | | | | | | |

# Working in the Cloud

**CASE** ▶ In your job for the Vancouver branch of Quest Specialty Travel, you travel frequently, you often work from home, and you also collaborate online with colleagues and clients. You want to learn how you can use SkyDrive with Office 2013 to work in the Cloud so that you can access and work on your files anytime and anywhere. (*Note*: SkyDrive and Office Web Apps are dynamic Web pages, and might change over time, including the way they are organized and how commands are performed. The steps and figures in this appendix reflect these pages at the time this book was published.)

## Unit Objectives

After completing this unit, you will be able to:

- Understand Office 2013 in the Cloud
- Work Online
- Explore SkyDrive
- Manage Files on SkyDrive
- Share Files
- Explore Office Web Apps
- Complete a Team Project

## Files You Will Need

WEB-1.pptx
WEB-2.docx

# Understand Office 2013 in the Cloud

The term **cloud computing** refers to the process of working with files and apps online. You may already be familiar with Web-based e-mail accounts such as Gmail and outlook.com. These applications are **cloud-based**, which means that you do not need a program installed on your computer to run them. Office 2013 has also been designed as a cloud-based application. When you work in Office 2013, you can choose to store your files "in the cloud" so that you can access them on any device connected to the Internet. **CASE** ➤ *You review the concepts related to working online with Office 2013.*

## DETAILS

- ### How does Office 2013 work in the Cloud?

  When you launch an Office application such as Word or Excel, you might see your name and maybe even your picture in the top right corner of your screen. This information tells you that you have signed in to Office 2013, either with your personal account or with an account you are given as part of an organization such as a company or school. When you are signed in to Office and click the FILE tab in any Office 2013 application such as Word or Excel, you see a list of the files that you have used recently on your current computer and on any other connected device such as a laptop, a tablet or even a Windows phone. The file path appears beneath each filename so that you can quickly identify its location as shown in **FIGURE WEB-1**. Office 2013 also remembers your personalized settings so that they are available on all the devices you use.

- ### What are roaming settings?

  A **roaming setting** is a setting that travels with you on every connected device. Examples of roaming settings include your personal settings such as your name and picture, the files you've used most recently, your list of connected services such as Facebook and Twitter, and any custom dictionaries you've created. Two particularly useful roaming settings are the Word Resume Reading Position setting and the PowerPoint Last Viewed Slide setting. For example, when you open a PowerPoint presentation that you've worked on previously, you will see a message similar to the one shown in **FIGURE WEB-2**.

- ### What is SkyDrive?

  **SkyDrive** is an online storage and file sharing service. When you are signed in to your computer with your Microsoft account, you receive access to your own SkyDrive, which is your personal storage area on the Internet. On your SkyDrive, you are given space to store up to 7 GB of data online. A SkyDrive location is already created on your computer as shown in **FIGURE WEB-3**. Every file you save to SkyDrive is synced among your computers and your personal storage area on SkyDrive.com. The term **synced** (which stands for synchronized) means that when you add, change or delete files on one computer, the same files on your other devices are also updated.

- ### What are Office Web Apps?

  **Office Web Apps** are versions of Microsoft Word, Excel, PowerPoint, and OneNote that you can access online from your SkyDrive. An Office Web App does not include all of the features and functions included with the full Office version of its associated application. However, you can use the Office Web App from any computer that is connected to the Internet, even if Microsoft Office 2013 is not installed on that computer.

- ### How do SkyDrive and Office Web Apps work together?

  You can create a file in Office 2013 using Word, Excel, PowerPoint, or OneNote and then save it to your SkyDrive. You can then open the Office file saved to SkyDrive and edit it using your Office 2013 apps. If you do not have Office 2013 installed on the computer you are using, you can edit the file using your Web browser and the corresponding Office Web App. You can also use an Office Web App to create a new file, which is saved automatically to SkyDrive while you work and you can download a file created with an Office Web App and work with the file in the full version of the corresponding Office application.

**FIGURE WEB-1:** FILE tab in Microsoft Excel

**FIGURE WEB-2:** PowerPoint Last Viewed Slide setting

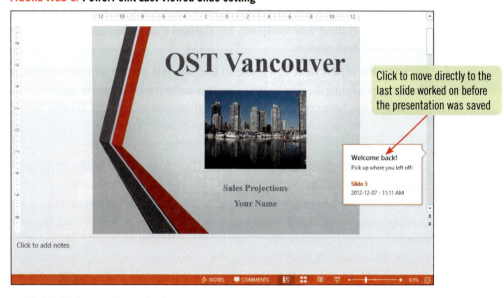

**FIGURE WEB-3:** Saving a Word file on SkyDrive

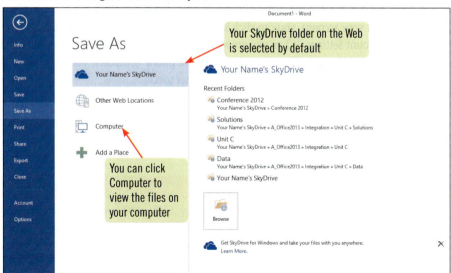

# Explore SkyDrive

**Learning Outcomes**
- Save a file to SkyDrive
- Create a folder on SkyDrive

SkyDrive works like the hard drive on your computer. You can save and open files from SkyDrive, create folders, and manage your files. You can access the files you save on SkyDrive from any of your connected devices and from anywhere you have a computer connection. **CASE** *You open a PowerPoint presentation, save the file to your SkyDrive, then create a folder.*

## STEPS

1. **Start PowerPoint, then open the file WEB-1.pptx from the location where you store your Data Files**

**QUICK TIP**

If you are signed in with your own account, you will see Your Name's Sky-Drive (for example, "Tom's SkyDrive").

2. **Click the FILE tab, click Save As, then click Your Name's SkyDrive (top selection) if it is not already selected**

3. **Click the Browse button**

   The Save As dialog box opens, showing the folders stored on your SkyDrive. You may have several folders already stored there or you may have none.

4. **Click New folder, type Cengage, then press [Enter]**

5. **Double-click Cengage, select WEB-1.pptx in the File name text box, type WEB-QST Vancouver 1 as shown in FIGURE WEB-6, then click Save**

   The file is saved to the Cengage folder on the SkyDrive that is associated with your Microsoft account. The PowerPoint window reappears.

6. **Click the FILE tab, click Close, click the FILE tab, then click Open**

   WEB-QST Vancouver 1.pptx appears as the first file listed in the Recent Presentations list, and the path to your Cengage folder on your SkyDrive appears beneath it.

7. **Click WEB-QST Vancouver 1.pptx to open it, then type your name where indicated on the title slide**

8. **Click Slide 2 in the Navigation pane, select 20% in the third bullet, type 30%, click the FILE tab, click Save As, click Cengage under Current Folder, change the file name to WEB-QST Vancouver 2, then click Save**

9. **Exit PowerPoint**

   A new version of the presentation is saved to the Cengage folder that you created on SkyDrive.

---

### How to disable default saving to Skydrive

You can specify how you want to save files from Office 2013 applications. By default, files are saved to locations you specify on your SkyDrive. You can change the default to be a different location. In Word, PowerPoint, or Excel, click the FILE tab, then click Options. Click Save in the left sidebar, then in the Save section, click the Save to Computer by default check box, as shown in **FIGURE WEB-7**. Click OK to close the PowerPoint Options dialog box. The Save options you've selected will be active in Word, PowerPoint, and Excel, regardless of which application you were using when you changed the option.

**FIGURE WEB-6:** Saving a presentation to SkyDrive

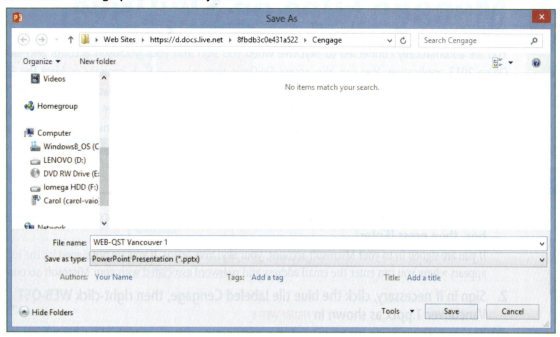

**FIGURE WEB-7:** Changing the default Save location in PowerPoint

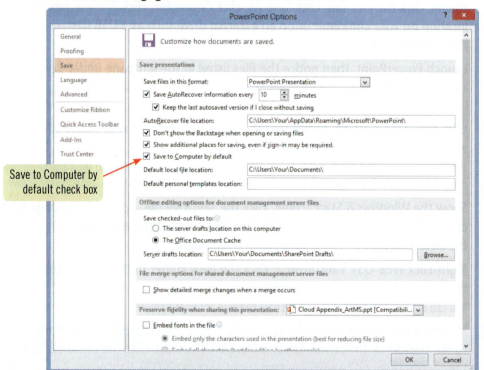

# Share Files

One of the great advantages of working with SkyDrive is that you can share your files with others. Suppose, for example, that you want a colleague to review a presentation you created in PowerPoint and then add a new slide. You can, of course, e-mail the presentation directly to your colleague who can then make changes and e-mail the presentation back. Alternatively, you can share the PowerPoint file directly from SkyDrive. Your colleague can edit the file using the PowerPoint Web App or the full version of PowerPoint, and then you can check the updated file on SkyDrive. In this way, you and your colleague are working with just one version of the presentation that you both can update. **CASE** *You have decided to share files in the Illustrated folder that you created in the previous lesson with another individual. You start by sharing files with your partner and your partner can share files with you.*

## STEPS

1. Identify a partner with whom you can work, and obtain his or her e-mail address; you can choose someone in your class or someone on your e-mail list, but it should be someone who will be completing these steps when you are

2. Right-click the Illustrated folder, then click Sharing as shown in FIGURE WEB-10

3. Type the e-mail address of your partner

4. Click in the Include a personal message box, then type Here's the presentation we're working on together as shown in FIGURE WEB-11

5. Verify that the Recipients can edit check box is selected, then click Share

   Your partner will receive a message advising him or her that you have shared the WEB-QST Vancouver 2.pptx file. If your partner is completing the steps at the same time, you will receive an e-mail from your partner.

6. Check your e-mail for a message advising you that your partner has shared a folder with you

   The subject of the e-mail message will be "[Name] has shared documents with you."

7. If you have received the e-mail, click the Show content link that appears in the warning box, if necesary, then click WEB-QST Vancouver 2.pptx in the body of the e-mail message

   The PowerPoint presentation opens in the Microsoft PowerPoint Web App. You will work in the Web App in the next lesson.

---

### Co-authoring documents

You can work on a document, presentation, or workbook simultaneously with a partner. First, save the file to your SkyDrive. Click the FILE tab, click Share, then click Invite People. Enter the email addresses of the people you want to work on the file with you and then click Share. Once your partner has received, opened, and started editing the document, you can start working together. You will see a notification in the status bar that someone is editing the document with you. When you click the notification, you can see the name of the other user and their picture if they have one attached to their Windows account. When your partner saves, you'll see his or changes in green shading which goes away the next time you save. You'll have an opportunity to co-author documents when you complete the Team Project at the end of this appendix.

**FIGURE WEB-10:** Sharing a file from SkyDrive

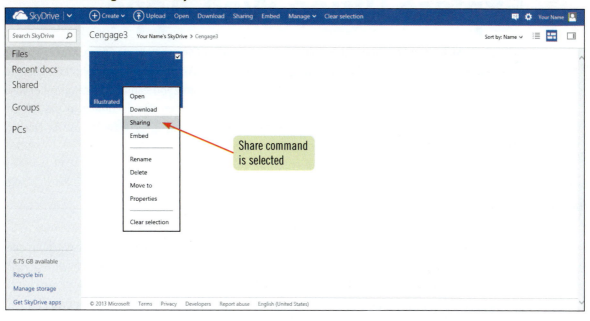

**FIGURE WEB-11:** Sharing a file with another person

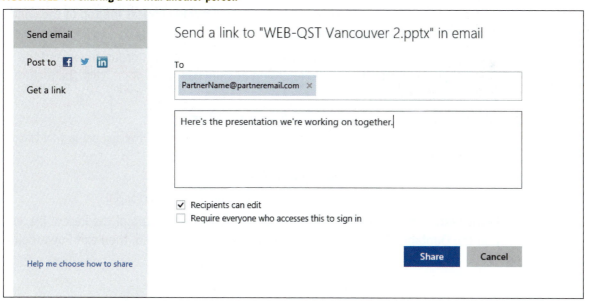

# Explore Office Web Apps

As you have learned, a Web App is a scaled-down version of an Office program. Office Web Apps include Word, Excel, PowerPoint, and OneNote. You can use the Office Web Apps to create and edit documents even if you don't have Office 2013 installed on your computer and you can use them on other devices such as tablets and smartphones. From SkyDrive, you can also open the document in the full Office application if the application is installed on the computer you are using. **CASE** ▶ *You use the PowerPoint Web App and the full version of PowerPoint to edit the presentation.*

## STEPS

1. Click **EDIT PRESENTATION**, then click **Edit in PowerPoint Web App**

   Presentations opened using the PowerPoint Web App have the same look and feel as presentations opened using the full version of PowerPoint. However, like all of the Office Web Apps, the PowerPoint Web App has fewer features available than the full version of PowerPoint.

2. Review the Ribbon and its tabs to familiarize yourself with the commands you can access from the PowerPoint Web App

   **TABLE WEB-1** summarizes the commands that are available.

3. Click **Slide 3**, click the text **Hornby Island**, click it again and select it, then type **Tofino** so the bullet item reads **Tofino Sea Kayaking**

4. Click outside the text box, click the **DESIGN tab**, then click the **More Themes list arrow** ▼ to show the selection of designs available

   A limited number of designs are available on the PowerPoint Web App. When you want to use a design or a command that is not available on the PowerPoint Web App, you open the file in the full version of PowerPoint.

5. Click on a blank area of the slide, click **OPEN IN POWERPOINT** at the top of the window, then click **Yes** in response to the message

6. Click the **DESIGN tab**, click the **More button** ▼ in the Themes group to expand the Themes gallery, select the **Quotable design** as shown in **FIGURE WEB-12**, click the **picture** on Slide 1, then press **[Delete]**

7. Click the **Save button** 🖫 on the Quick Access toolbar

   The Save button includes a small icon indicating you are saving to SkyDrive and not to your computer's hard drive or an external drive.

8. Click the **Close button** ✖ to exit PowerPoint

   You open the document again to verify that your partner made the same changes.

9. Launch PowerPoint, click **WEB-QST Vancouver 2.pptx** at the top of the Recent list, verify that the Quotable design is applied and the picture is removed, then exit PowerPoint

---

### Exploring other Office Web Apps

Three other Office Web Apps are Word, Excel, and OneNote. You can share files on SkyDrive directly from any of these applications using the same method you used to share files from PowerPoint. To familiarize yourself with the commands available in an Office Web App, open the file and then review the commands on each tab on the Ribbon. If you want to perform a task that is not available in the Web App, open the file in the full version of the application.

**FIGURE WEB-12:** Selecting the Quotable design

**TABLE WEB-1:** Commands on the PowerPoint Web App

| tab | category/group | options |
|---|---|---|
| FILE | Info | • Open in PowerPoint (also available on the toolbar above the document window) |
| | | • Previous Versions |
| | Save As | • Where's the Save Button?: In PowerPoint Web App, the presentation is being saved automatically so there is no Save button |
| | | • Download: use to download a copy of the presentation to your computer |
| | Print | • Create a printable PDF of the presentation that you can then open and print |
| | Share | • Share with people - you can invite others to view and edit your presentation |
| | | • Embed - include the presentation in a blog on Web site |
| | About | • Try Microsoft Office, Terms of Use, and Privacy and Cookies |
| | Help | • Help with PowerPoint questions, Give Feedback to Microsoft, and modify how you can view the presentation (for example, text only) |
| | Exit | • Close the presentation and exit to view SkyDrive folders |
| HOME | Clipboard | • Cut, Copy, Paste, Format Painter |
| | Delete | • Delete a slide |
| | Slides | • Add a new slide, duplicate a slide, hide a slide |
| | Font | • Change the font, size, style, and color of selected text |
| | Paragraph | • Add bullets and numbering, indent text, align text, and change text direction |
| | Drawing | • Add text boxes and shapes, arrange them on the slide, apply Quick Styles, modify shape fill and outline, and duplicate a shape |
| INSERT | Slides | • Add new slides with selected layout |
| | Images | • Add pictures from your computer, online pictures, or screen shots |
| | Illustrations | • Add shapes, SmartArt, or charts |
| | Links | • Add links or actions to objects |
| | Text | • Add comments, text boxes, headers and footers, and other text elements |
| | Comments | • Add comments |
| DESIGN | Themes | • Apply a limited number of themes to a presentation and apply variants to a selected theme |
| | | • Apply variants to a selected theme |
| ANIMATIONS | Animation | • Apply a limited number of animation effects to a slide element and modify existing timings |
| TRANSITIONS | Transitions to This Slide | • Apply a limited number of transition effects to slides and chose to apply the effect to all slides |
| VIEW | Presentation Views | • You can view the slide in Editing View, Reading View, Slide Show View, and Notes View and you can show any comments made by users who worked on PowerPoint using the full version |

Cloud

# Team Project

## Introduction

From SkyDrive, you can easily collaborate with others to produce documents, presentations, and spreadsheets that include each user's input. Instead of emailing a document to colleagues and then waiting for changes, you can both work on the document at the same time online. To further explore how you can work with SkyDrive and Office 2013, you will work with two other people to complete a team project. The subject of the team project is the planning of a special event of your choice, such as a class party, a lecture, or a concert. The special event should be limited to a single afternoon or evening.

Follow the guidelines provided below to create the files required for the team project. When you have completed the project, the team will submit a Word document containing information about your project, as well as three files related to the project: a Word document, a PowerPoint presentation, and an Excel workbook.

## Project Setup

### As a team, work together to complete the following tasks.

a. Share email addresses among all three team members.

b. Set up a time (either via email, an online chat session, Internet Messaging, or face to face) when you will get together to choose your topic and assign roles.

c. At your meeting, complete the table below with information about your team and your special event.

| |
| --- |
| **Team Name** (last name of one team member or another name that describes the project.) |
| **Team Members** |
| **Event type** (for example, party, lecture, concert, etc.) |
| **Event purpose** (for example, fundraiser for a specific cause, celebrate the end of term, feature a special guest, etc.) |
| **Event location, date, and time** |
| **Team Roles** indicate who is responsible for each of the following three files (one file per team member) |
| **Word document:** |
| **Excel workbook:** |
| **PowerPoint presentation:** |

## Document Development

Individually, complete the tasks listed below for the file you are responsible for. You need to develop appropriate content, format the file attractively, and then be prepared to share the file with the other team members.

### Word Document

The Word document contains a description of your special event and includes a table listing responsibilities and a time line. Create the Word document as follows:

1. Create a Cloud Project folder on your SkyDrive, then create a new Word document and save it as **Cloud Project_ Word Description** to the Cloud Project folder.

# Document Development (continued)

2. Include a title with the name of your project and a subtitle with the names of your team members. Format the title with the Title style and the subtitle with the Subtitle style.

3. Write a paragraph describing the special event—its topics, purpose, the people involved, etc. You can paraphrase some of the information your team discussed in your meeting.

4. Create a table similar to the table shown below and then complete it with the required information. Include up to ten rows. A task could be "Contact the caterers" or "Pick up the speaker." Visualize the sequence of tasks required to put on the event.

| Task | Person Responsible | Deadline |
|------|--------------------|----------|
|      |                    |          |
|      |                    |          |

5. Format the table using the table style of your choice.

6. Save the document to your SkyDrive. You will share the document with your team members and receive feedback in the next section.

## Excel Workbook

The Excel workbook contains a budget for the special event. Create the Excel workbook as follows:

1. Create a new Excel workbook and save it as **Cloud Project_Excel Budget** to the Cloud Project folder on your SkyDrive.

2. Create a budget that includes both the revenues you expect from the event (for example, ticket sales, donations, etc.) and the expenses. Expense items include advertising costs (posters, ads, etc.), food costs if the event is catered, transportation costs, etc. The revenues and expenses you choose will depend upon the nature of the project.

3. Make the required calculations to total all the revenue items and all the expense items.

4. Calculate the net profit (or loss) as the revenue minus the expenses.

5. Format the budget attractively using fill colors, border lines, and other enhancements to make the data easy to read.

6. Save the workbook to your SkyDrive. You will share the workbook with your team members and receive feedback in the next section.

## PowerPoint Presentation

The PowerPoint presentation contains a presentation that describes the special event to an audience who may be interested in attending. Create the PowerPoint presentation as follows:

1. Create a new PowerPoint presentation and save it as **Cloud Project_PowerPoint Presentation** to the Cloud Project folder on your SkyDrive.

2. Create a presentation that consists of five slides including the title slide as follows:

   a. Slide 1: Title slide includes the name of the event and your team members

   b. Slide 2: Purpose of the party or event

   c. Slide 3: Location, time, and cost

   d. Slide 4: Chart showing a breakdown of costs (to be supplied when you co-author in the next section)

   e. Slide 5: Motivational closing slide designed to encourage the audience to attend; include appropriate pictures

3. Format the presentation attractively using the theme of your choice.

4. Save the presentation to your SkyDrive. You will share the presentation with your team members and receive feedback.

# Co-Authoring on Skydrive

You need to share your file, add feedback to the other two files, then create a final version of your file. When you read the file created by the other two team members, you need to add additional data or suggestions. For example, if you created the Excel budget, you can provide the person who created the PowerPoint presentation with information about the cost break-down. If you created the Word document, you can add information about the total revenue and expenses contained in the Excel budget to your description. You decide what information to add to each of the two files you work with.

1. Open the file you created.
2. Click the **FILE tab**, click **Share**, then click **Invite People**.
3. Enter the email addresses of the other two team members, then enter the following message: **Here's the file I created for our team project. Please make any changes, provide suggestions, and then save it. Thanks!** See **FIGURE WEB-13**.

**FIGURE WEB-13**

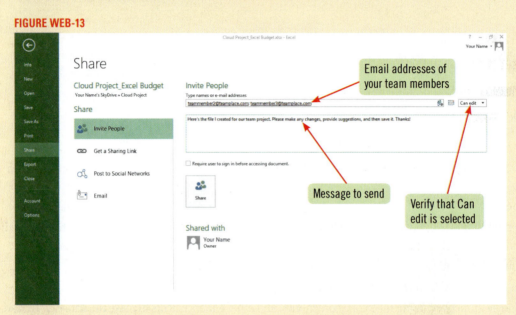

4. Click the **Share button**.
5. Allow team members time to add information and comments to your file. Team members should save frequently. When the file is saved, it is saved directly to your SkyDrive. Note that you can work together on the document or you can work separately. You can also choose to make changes with the full version of the Office 2013 applications or with the Office Web Apps. When someone is working on your file, you will see their user name on the status bar.
6. Decide which changes you want to keep, make any further changes you think are needed to make the document as clear as possible, then save a final version.

# Project Summary

When you are pleased with the contents of your file and have provided feedback to your team members, assign a team member to complete the following tasks and then complete your portion as required.

1. Open **WEB-2.docx** from the location where you save your Data Files, then save it to your Cloud Project folder on your SkyDrive as **Cloud Project_Summary**.
2. Read the directions in the document, then enter your name as Team Member 1 and write a short description of your experience working with SkyDrive and Office 2013 to complete the team project.
3. Share the file with your team members and request that they add their own names and descriptions.
4. When all team members have finished working on the document, save all the changes.
5. Make sure you store all four files completed for the project in the Cloud Project appendix on your SkyDrive, then submit them to your instructor on behalf of your team.

# Glossary

**3-D reference** A worksheet reference that uses values on other sheets or workbooks, effectively creating another dimension to a workbook.

**A**bsolute cell reference In a formula, a cell address that refers to a specific cell and does not change when you copy the formula; indicated by a dollar sign before the column letter and/or row number. *See also* Relative cell reference.

**Active** The currently available document, program, or object; on the taskbar, when more than one program is open, the button for the active program appears slightly lighter.

**Active cell** The cell in which you are currently working.

**Alignment** The placement of cell contents in relation to a cell's edges; for example, left-aligned, centered, or right-aligned.

**Argument** Information necessary for a formula or function to calculate an answer.

**Arithmetic operators** In a formula, symbols that perform mathematical calculations, such as addition (+), subtraction (–), multiplication (*), division (/), or exponentiation (^).

**AutoFill** Feature activated by dragging the fill handle; copies a cell's contents or continues a series of entries into adjacent cells.

**AutoFill Options button** Button that appears after using the fill handle to copy cell contents; enables you to choose to fill cells with specific elements (such as formatting) of the copied cell if desired.

**AutoFit** A feature that automatically adjusts the width of a column or the height of a row to accommodate its widest or tallest entry.

**B**ackstage view Appears when then FILE tab is clicked. The navigation bar on the left side contains commands to perform actions common to most Office programs, such as opening a file, saving a file, and closing the file.

**Backward-compatible** Software feature that enables documents saved in an older version of a program to be opened in a newer version of the program.

**C**alculation operators Symbols in a formula that indicate what type of calculation to perform on the cells, ranges, or values.

**Category axis** Horizontal axis in a chart, usually containing the names of data categories; in a 2-dimensional chart, also known as the x-axis.

**Cell** The intersection of a column and a row in a worksheet or table.

**Cell address** The location of a cell, expressed by cell coordinates; for example, the cell address of the cell in column A, row 1 is A1.

**Cell pointer** Dark rectangle that outlines the active cell.

**Cell styles** Predesigned combinations of formats based on themes that can be applied to selected cells to enhance the look of a worksheet.

**Chart sheet** A separate sheet in a workbook that contains only a chart, which is linked to the workbook data.

**Charts** Pictorial representations of worksheet data that make it easier to see patterns, trends, and relationships; also called graphs.

**Clip** A media file, such as a graphic, sound, animation, or movie.

**Clip art** A graphic image, such as a corporate logo, a picture, or a photo, that can be inserted into a document.

**Clipboard** A temporary Windows storage area that holds the selections you copy or cut.

**Cloud computing** Work done in a virtual environment using data, applications, and resources stored on servers and accessed over the Internet or a company's internal network rather than on users' computers.

**Column heading** Box that appears above each column in a worksheet; identifies the column letter, such as A, B, etc.

**Combination chart** Two charts in one, such as a column chart combined with a line chart, that together graph related but dissimilar data.

**Comparison operators** In a formula, symbols that compare values for the purpose of true/false results.

**Compatibility** The ability of different programs to work together and exchange data.

**Complex formula** A formula that uses more than one arithmetic operator.

**Conditional formatting** A type of cell formatting that changes based on the cell's value or the outcome of a formula.

**Consolidate** To combine data on multiple worksheets and display the result on another worksheet.

**Contextual tab** A tab that is displayed only when a specific task can be performed: they appear in an accent color and close when no longer needed.

**D**ata marker A graphical representation of a data point in a chart, such as a bar or column.

**Data point** Individual piece of data plotted in a chart.

**Data series** The selected range in a worksheet whose related data points Excel converts into a chart.

**Delimiter** A separator such as a space, comma, or semicolon between elements in imported data.

**Dialog box launcher** An icon you can click to open a dialog box or task pane from which to choose related commands.

**Document window** Most of the screen in any given program, where you create a document, slide, or worksheet.

**E**dit To make a change to the contents of an active cell.

**Electronic spreadsheet** A computer program used to perform calculations and analyze and present numeric data.

**Embedded chart** A chart displayed as an object in a worksheet.

**Exploding** Visually pulling a slice of a pie chart away from the whole pie chart in order to add emphasis to the pie slice.

**External reference indicator** The exclamation point (!) used in a formula to indicate that a referenced cell is outside the active sheet.

**F**ile A stored collection of data.

**Flash Fill** An Excel feature that automatically fills in column or row data based on calculations you enter.

**Font** The typeface or design of a set of characters (letters, numbers, symbols, and punctuation marks).

**Font size** The size of characters, measured in units called points.

**Font style** Format such as bold, italic, and underlining that can be applied to change the way characters look in a worksheet or chart.

**Format** The appearance of a cell and its contents, including font, font styles, font color, fill color, borders, and shading. *See also* Number format.

**Formula** A set of instructions used to perform one or more numeric calculations, such as adding, multiplying, or averaging, on values or cells.

**Formula bar** The area above the worksheet grid where you enter or edit data in the active cell.

**Formula prefix** An arithmetic symbol, such as the equal sign (=), used to start a formula.

**Function** A special, predefined formula that provides a shortcut for a commonly used or complex calculation, such as SUM (for calculating a sum) or FV (for calculating the future value of an investment).

**G**allery A visual collection of choices you can browse through to make a selection. Often available with Live Preview.

**Gridlines** Evenly spaced horizontal and/or vertical lines used in a worksheet or chart to make it easier to read.

**Groups** Each tab on the Ribbon is arranged into groups to make features easy to find.

**I**nsertion point A blinking vertical line that appears when you click in the formula bar or in an active cell; indicates where new text will be inserted.

**Integrate** To incorporate a document and parts of a document created in one program into another program; for example, to

incorporate an Excel chart into a PowerPoint slide, or an Access table into a Word document.

**Interface** The look and feel of a program; for example, the appearance of commands and the way they are organized in the program window.

**L**abels Descriptive text or other information that identifies data in rows, columns, or charts, but is not included in calculations.

**Landscape** Page orientation in which the contents of a page span the length of a page rather than its width, making the page wider than it is tall.

**Launch** To open or start a program on your computer.

**Legend** In a chart, information that identifies how data is represented by colors or patterns.

**Linking** The dynamic referencing of data in the same or in other workbooks, so that when data in the other location is changed, the references in the current location are automatically updated.

**Live Preview** A feature that lets you point to a choice in a gallery or palette and see the results in the document without actually clicking the choice.

**Logical test** The first part of an IF function; if the logical test is true, then the second part of the function is applied; if it is false, then the third part of the function is applied.

**M**ajor gridlines In a chart, the gridlines that represent the values at the tick marks on the value axis.

**Minor gridlines** In a chart, the gridlines that represent the values between the tick marks on the value axis.

**Mixed reference** Cell reference that combines both absolute and relative cell addressing.

**Mode indicator** An area on the left end of the status bar that indicates the program's status. For example, when you are changing the contents of a cell, the word 'Edit' appears in the mode indicator.

**N**ame box Box to the left of the formula bar that shows the cell reference or name of the active cell.

**Navigate** To move around in a worksheet; for example, you can use the arrow keys on the keyboard to navigate from cell to cell, or press [Page Up] or [Page Down] to move one screen at a time.

**Normal view** Default worksheet view that shows the worksheet without features such as headers and footers; ideal for creating and editing a worksheet, but may not be detailed enough when formatting a document.

**Number format** A format applied to values to express numeric concepts, such as currency, date, and percentage.

**O**bject Independent element on a worksheet (such as a chart or graphic) that is not located in a specific cell or range; can be moved and resized and displays handles when selected.

**Office Web Apps** Versions of the Microsoft Office applications with limited functionality that are available online. Users can view documents online and then edit them in the browser using a selection of functions. Office Web Apps are available for Word, PowerPoint, Excel, and One Note.

**Online collaboration** The ability to incorporate feedback or share information across the Internet or a company network or intranet.

**Order of precedence** Rules that determine the order in which operations are performed within a formula containing more than one arithmetic operator.

**P**age Break Preview A worksheet view that displays a reduced view of each page in your worksheet, along with page break indicators that you can drag to include more or less information on a page.

**Page Layout view** Provides an accurate view of how a worksheet will look when printed, including headers and footers.

**Paste Options button** Button that appears onscreen after pasting content; enables you to choose to paste only specific elements of the copied selection, such as the formatting or values, if desired.

**Plot area** In a chart, the area inside the horizontal and vertical axes.

**Point** A unit of measure used for font size and row height. One point is equal to 1/72nd of an inch.

**Portrait** Page orientation in which the contents of a page span the width of a page, so the page is taller than it is wide.

**Previewing** Prior to printing, seeing onscreen exactly how the printed document will look.

**Print area** The portion of a worksheet that will be printed; can be defined by selecting a range and then using the Print Area button on the Page Layout tab.

**Q**uick Access toolbar A small toolbar on the left side of a Microsoft application program window's title bar, containing icons that you click to quickly perform common actions, such as saving a file.

**Quick Analysis tool** An icon that is displayed below and to the right of a range that lets you easily create charts and other elements.

**R**ange A selection of two or more cells, such as B5:B14.

**Reference operators** In a formula, symbols which enable you to use ranges in calculations.

**Relative cell reference** In a formula, a cell address that refers to a cell's location in relation to the cell containing the formula and that automatically changes to reflect the new location when the formula is copied or moved; default type of referencing used in Excel worksheets. *See also* Absolute cell reference.

**Return** In a function, to display a result.

**Ribbon** Appears beneath the title bar in every Office program window, and displays commands you're likely to need for the current task.

**S**cope In a named cell or range, the worksheet(s) in which the name can be used.

**Screen capture** An electronic snapshot of your screen, as if you took a picture of it with a camera, which you can paste into a document.

**Scroll bars** Bars on the right edge (vertical scroll bar) and bottom edge (horizontal scroll bar) of the document window that allow you to move around in a document that is too large to fit on the screen at once.

**Secondary axis** In a combination chart, an additional axis that supplies the scale for one of the chart types used.

**Sheet tabs** Identify the sheets in a workbook and let you switch between sheets; located below the worksheet grid.

**Sheet tab scrolling buttons** Allow you to navigate to additional sheet tabs when available; located to the left of the sheet tabs.

**Sizing handles** Small series of dots at the corners and edges of a chart indicating that the chart is selected; drag to resize the chart.

**SkyDrive** An online storage and file sharing service. Access to SkyDrive is through a Microsoft account. Up to 25 GB of data can be stored in a personal SkyDrive, with each file a maximum size of 300 MB.

**SmartArt graphics** Predesigned diagram types for the following types of data: List, Process, Cycle, Hierarchy, Relationship, Matrix, and Pyramid.

**Sparkline** A quick, simple chart located within a cell that serves as a visual indicator of data trends.

**Stated conditions** In a logical formula, criteria you create.

**Status bar** Bar at the bottom of the Excel window that provides a brief description about the active command or task in progress.

**Suite** A group of programs that are bundled together and share a similar interface, making it easy to transfer skills and program content among them.

**T**able An organized collection of rows and columns of similarly structured data on a worksheet.

**Table styles** Predesigned formatting that can be applied to a range of cells or even to an entire worksheet; especially useful for those ranges with labels in the left column and top row, and totals in the bottom row or right column. *See also* Table.

**Tabs** Organizational unit used for commands on the Ribbon. The tab names appear at the top of the Ribbon and the active tab appears in front.

**Template** A predesigned, formatted file that serves as the basis for a new workbook; Excel template files have the file extension .xltx.

**Text annotations** Labels added to a chart to draw attention to or describe a particular area.

**Text concatenation operators** In a formula, symbols used to join strings of text in different cells.

**Theme** A predefined set of colors, fonts, line and fill effects, and other formats that can be applied to an Excel worksheet and give it a consistent, professional look.

**Tick marks** Notations of a scale of measure on a chart axis.

**Title bar** Appears at the top of every Office program window: displays the document name and program name.

**U**ser interface A collective term for all the ways you interact with a software program.

**V**alue axis In a chart, the axis that contains numerical values; in a 2-dimensional chart, also known as the y-axis.

**Values** Numbers, formulas, and functions used in calculations.

**View** A method of displaying a document window to show more or fewer details or a different combination of elements that makes it easier to complete certain tasks, such as formatting or reading text.

**W**hat-if analysis A decision-making tool in which data is changed and formulas are recalculated, in order to predict various possible outcomes.

**Workbook** A collection of related worksheets contained within a single file which has the file extension xlsx.

**Worksheet** A single sheet within a workbook file; also, the entire area within an electronic spreadsheet that contains a grid of columns and rows.

**Worksheet window** Area of the program window that displays part of the current worksheet; the worksheet window displays only a small fraction of the worksheet, which can contain a total of 1,048,576 rows and 16,384 columns.

**X**-axis The horizontal axis in a chart; because it often shows data categories, such as months or locations, also called Category axis.

**XML** Acronym that stands for eXtensible Markup Language, which is a language used to structure, store, and send information.

**Y**-axis The vertical axis in a chart; because it often shows numerical values, also called Value axis.

**Z**-axis The third axis in a true 3-D chart, lets you compare data points across both categories and values.

**Zooming in** A feature that makes a document appear larger but shows less of it on screen at once; does not affect actual document size.

**Zooming out** A feature that shows more of a document on screen at once but at a reduced size; does not affect actual document size.

# Index